THOMAS HEYWOOD

Engraving prefixed to " The Seraphim," Book I of *The Hierarchy of the Blessed Angels*, with Delphi and Jerusalem in the background.

Thomas Heywood

by

FREDERICK S. BOAS
LL.D., D.LITT., F.R.S.L.

PHAETON PRESS

NEW YORK

1975

Originally Published 1950
Reprinted 1975

Library of Congress Cataloging in Publication Data

Boas, Frederick Samuel, 1862-1957.
    Thomas Heywood.

    Reprint of the 1950 ed. published by Williams &
Norgate, London.
    1. Heywood, Thomas, d. 1641--Criticism and interpre-
tation.
[PR2576.B6   1975]   822'.3   75-15587
ISBN 0-87753-056-4

CONTENTS

ILLUSTRATIONS

PREFACE

The scope of this book is indicated by its sub-title, "A Selective Study!" It does not purport to be a full-length survey of the whole of Thomas Heywood's writings, and an adequately documented inquiry into the problems of their canon and chronology. For these reference should be made to Dr. A. Melville Clark's volume *Thomas Heywood : Playwright and Miscellanist* (Blackwell, 1931), to which students of Heywood, even if they may not accept all his conclusions, are deeply indebted.

My aim, within a general sketch of Heywood's very varied achievement, has been to draw attention to those of his works which are comparatively unfamiliar to most readers. These include his two long and important poems *Troia Britannica* and *The Hierarchy of the Blessed Angels*, and his prose *History of Women*, Γυναικεῖον, which, so far as I know, have never been reprinted. They also comprise some of his earlier plays, *King Edward the Fourth* and *The Four Prentices of London*, his classical dramas in *The Four Ages*, his *Pleasant Dialogues and Dramas*, and his London Mayoral Pageants, which are only accessible in Pearson's reprints (1874), or some of them in the Shakespeare Society's editions (1842 and 1851), or *Pleasant Dialogues and Dramas* in W. Bang's *Materialen*, iii.

To these less known writings of Heywood, in verse, prose or dramatic form I have given special space, with liberal quotations, in the hope that I may be able to communicate to other readers some of the interest that

I have felt in them myself. They are essential to a full valuation of his achievement.

In my quotations, except in some cases of rhyme, I have modernised the spelling and punctuation. I have to thank the Secretary of the Oxford University Press for allowing me to make use of some passages on Heywood in my *Introduction to Stuart Drama*, and the authorities of the British Museum for leave to reproduce, for the first time, some of the title-pages and engravings in Heywood's volumes.

F.S.B.

CHAPTER 1

Early Years—Chronicle-History Plays

The leading Elizabethan dramatists may from one point of view be divided into two groups. There are those whose only connection with the professional stage was as playwrights. Amongst these were Kyd and Marlowe, Beaumont and Fletcher, Middleton and Massinger, Webster and Ford, Tourneur and Shirley. Another group combined the roles of actor and playwright. It is headed by Shakespeare and included Jonson (in his earlier days), William Rowley, Nathan Field, Richard Brome and Thomas Heywood.

It was probably lack of means, though he came of reputable stock and was well educated, that drove Heywood on to the boards. The date of his birth is uncertain but it was probably between July 1573 and the end of 1575. He himself stated several times that he was a native of Lincolnshire. The researches of Dr. A. M. Clark have made a strong case for his being a son of the Rev. Robert Heywood, rector of Rothwell and of Ashby-cum-Fenby in the deanery of Grimsby, 1575–93. This cleric was a member of an ancient Cheshire family and seems to have been a migrant into Lincolnshire. By his wife Elizabeth he had at least ten children younger than Thomas, which may account for his straitened circumstances. In his will, in which he makes among other bequests " two ewes and twoe Lambes, my new freese coate " and " my gray ambling nagge " he spoke of his " pore children." He had been able however to send his son Thomas to the university, for Heywood in his tract *An Apology for Actors* speaks of " the time of my residence in Cambridge, where I have seen tragedies, comedies, histories, pastorals and shows publicly acted." Dr. Clark has plausibly suggested that he may himself have had his first practice as an actor there. A statement by W. Cartwright in republishing the *Apology* in 1658 that Heywood had been a Fellow of Peterhouse is now discredited, though it has helped to account for a modern Master of that college, Sir A. W. Ward's special interest in him. He is likely to have been the Thomas Heywood who entered Emmanuel College, as a pensioner about 1591, when he was sixteen or seventeen. By his father's death in 1593 his academic career was probably cut short.

It is almost certain that he was the T. H. who signs the address to the " courteous readers " of *Œnone and Paris* entered in the Stationers' Register on 18th May, 1594, to the printer, Richard Jones. This poem of 804 lines is preserved in a unique copy, wanting the title-page, now in the Folger Shakespeare Library, Washington, whose late Director, Joseph Quincy Adams, published a reprint of it in 1943. In his introduction Adams showed conclusively that the poem was a patent imitation, the first that is known, of Shakespeare's *Venus and Adonis*. The theme in each case is parallel, a man coldly rejecting the pleas of a love-sick woman, and the setting is akin. The same six-lined stanza is used, and the echoes in wording and linagery are so flagrant that by modern standards they would amount to plagiarism.

Moreover, as Shakespeare had called *Venus and Adonis* " the first heir of my invention," so T.H. describes *Œnone and Paris* as " the first fruits of my endeavours and the maidenhead of my pen." This would exactly fit the earliest effort of a young impecunious Cantab, who like Marlowe, Greene and Nashe before him, had gone up to London to seek his fortune, and had sought to capture the town by an experiment in the erotic vein of poetry of which *Hero and Leander* and *Venus and Adonis* were triumphant examples. In support of the identification of T.H. with Thomas Heywood is the fact that throughout his career Heywood showed a passionate interest in the triangular love-story of Œnone-Paris-Helen. It was from Ovid's *Heroides* that he drew the main material for *Œnone and Paris*. He was later to translate from the same classical source the two epistles of " Paris to Helen " and " Helen to Paris," and to make use of them, somewhat incongruously, as Cantos 9 and 10 of his *Troia Britannica*. And in his dramatisation of the Paris-Helen story in *The Iron Age, Part I* he introduced, without classical precedent, a scene between Paris and Œnone, which recalls T.H.'s poem. Moreover in the " Judgement of Paris " episode T.H. is partly indebted to Lucian whose prose *Dialogue* on the subject, Heywood was later also to versify in *The Iron Age, Part I.*

With *Œnone and Paris* it is convenient to associate also Heywood's early translations of Ovid's *Ars Amatoria* and *Remedia Amoris*. In his preface to *The Brazen Age* (1613) he speaks of them as " things which out of juniority and want of judgement I committed to the view of some private friends, but with no purpose of publishing or further communicating them." A certain Austin, however, now a schoolmaster at Harrow, had borrowed from him the manuscripts, had them published and claimed most impudently that they were from his own pen.

Of two or three editions that appeared abroad of the translation of *Ars Amatoria* one was printed by Nicholas Iansz Visscher at Amsterdam and had an engraved title-page with Ovid instructing two sets of lovers in *Love's School*. Heywood with what was to be his characteristic economy of material was to make subsequent use of extracts from his translation in later works.

But though poetry might be a " side line " it was to the theatre that Heywood in London looked for a living. He took service with Philip Henslowe, manager and financier of the Lord Admiral's company, both as an actor and a journeyman playwright. Included is thirty shillings recorded by Henslowe in his *Diary* as lent to Edward Alleyn and three other actors since 14th October, 1596, is a sum lent unto them for " hawodes bocke," i.e., MS. of a play. Henslowe further records that on 25th March, 1598, " Thomas hawoode " hired himself, under a penalty of £40 for breach of contract, " not to playe any wher publicke a bowt london " for two years " but in my howsse." It is possible that after the two years he joined for a short period the Earl of Derby's company which performed *Edward IV*, but by the end of 1601 he was a sharer in the Earl of Worcester's company for there is a record in the Pipe Rolls of a payment to William Kempe and him for court performances by that company during the Christmas festivities of 1601–2 (3rd Jan. and 14th Feb.). By 17th August, 1602, this company were in relation with Henslowe, who opened an account for advances made for their play-books and apparel. He lent Heywood 2s. 6d. on 1st September, 1602, to buy " a payre of sylke garters." The company probably acted at the Rose.

Soon after the accession of James I the Earl of Worcester's company became the players of Queen Anne. Their names are given in a list including Thomas Haward among " officers to the Queen " who received 4½ yards of red cloth apiece for the coronation procession of 15th March, 1604. They were then playing at the Curtain in Holywell, to which a royal patent of 15th April, 1609 adds the Red Bull in Clerkenwell.

Heywood is mentioned in various later documents as a member of the Queen's Company, including their visit to Norwich in May, 1617. After her death on 2nd March, 1619, Thomas Heywood was fifth in the list of her company allowed black cloth to wear in her funeral procession. With the loss of her patronage the company, as a London organisation, appears soon to have disintegrated, and the last mention of Heywood as a Red Bull actor is an order of 3rd October, 1622, to him and five of his fellows to repair the highways near the theatre. In this odd connection twenty-four years after signing on with Henslowe, and nineteen before his death, he disappears as an actor.

There is no indication from any source what parts he played, either in his own or other men's plays, or whether he had special gifts as a performer. One need not take literally the statement by the bookseller, Francis Kirkman, in 1671, thirty years after his death, that he " acted almost every day." But no leading Elizabethan dramatist except Shakespeare had so continuous a professional connection with the stage.

Kirkman also stated that Heywood was so laborious that he " obliged himself to write a sheet every day, for several years together, but many of his plays being composed and written loosely in taverns, occasions them to be so mean." This again is a doubtful tradition but Heywood himself in the prefatory epistle to *The English Traveller*, in 1633, eight years before his death, claimed that there were 200 plays in which he had " either an entire hand or at least a main finger." This would seem an average of almost five plays a year. He also explained why they had not (like Ben Jonson's in 1616 or Shakespeare's in the First Folio of 1623) been published as *Works*. " One reason is, that many of them by shifting and change of Companies, have been negligently lost. Others of them are still retained in the hands of some actors, who think it against their peculiar profit to have them come in print, and a third, that it was never any great ambition in me, to be in this kind voluminously read."

Thus, only a relatively small proportion of his prolific dramatic output has survived and can be identified, though it is sufficient to give a reliable estimate of his capacity as a playwright and to illustrate his versatile achievement for the Tudor and Stuart stage. The first definite reference that we have to a play by him is Henslowe's payment quoted above, on October, 1596, for " hawodes bocke." On 6th December, 1598, Henslowe lent £3 to a representative of the Admiral's company to " bye a Booke called ware with out blowes and love with out sewte of Thomas hawodes." A further £2 was paid on 26th January when " stryfe " was substituted for " sewte " in the title. In February 1598–9 Henslowe again paid £5 for *Joan is as good as my Lady*, by Mr. Heywood, as he is now more ceremoniously called. These and probably other pieces have disappeared, but Heywood had by 1598 established sufficient reputation to be named by Francis Meres in *Wit's Treasury* among the best for comedy.

With the beginning of the new century in 1600 we get on to somewhat firmer ground. Marlowe and Shakespeare had raised the chronicle-history play into genuinely articulate dramatic form. With Heywood in his earlier ventures as a playwright it relapsed into the loosely jointed shape of the previous age. Though published anonymously in 1600, *The First and Second Parts of King Edward the Fourth*, " as it hath divers times been publicly played " by the servants of William Earl of Derby, is the earliest play in print which may be confidently attributed on internal evidence in whole or in part to Thomas Heywood. Of the medley of episodes strung together in this sprawling double drama there are several which bear his hall-mark. Though a Londoner only by residence, not by birth, he was an ardent devotee of the City and its traditions. Thus the earlier scenes of the play describe the rising under Thomas Nevile, Lord Falconbridge (a bastard like the earlier Falconbridge in Shakespeare's *King John*) in favour of the deposed Henry VI, which is defeated by the Lord Mayor at the head of London Volunteers. He appeals to them to be worthy of their ancestors :

> Think that in Richard's time, even such a rebel
> Was then by Walworth, the Lord Mayor of
>   London,
> Stabb'd dead in Smithfield.
> Then show yourselves, as it befits the time,
> And let this find a hundred Walworths now
> Dare stab a rebel, were he made of brass.
> And, prentices, stick to your officers,
> For you may come to be as we are now.

And one of the prentices cries in response :

> We have no tricks nor policies of war,
> But by the ancient custom of our fathers,
> We'll soundly lay it on, take't off that will.
> And London prentices, be rul'd by me :
> Die ere ye lose fair London's liberty.

In reward for their services King Edward knights Crosby, the Lord Mayor, and the Recorder, and offers the same honour to Matthew Shore, who declines it as unworthy, whereupon the King makes a promise that has afterwards a grimly ironical significance.

> Well, be it as thou wilt ; some other way
> We will devise to quittance thy deserts.

Shore, a goldsmith, is cousin to the Lord Mayor, who is a widower, and who asks Jane, Shore's wife, to act as Lady Mayoress when the King comes to dine with him. Edward, though newly married, at once becomes enamoured of her, visits Shore's shop in disguise which he throws off to avow his love, and at last by his importunity persuades her to come to Court as his mistress. But to retain for her the sympathies of the theatre-audience the dramatist shows her as using her influence on the King for benevolent purposes, and visiting once a week " the prisoners and the poor in hospitals."

To appreciate fully what follows, and what in more artistic form was to be the most distinctive contribution of Heywood to the Elizabethan stage, it has to be remembered that on that stage the " revenge " play had long been an established feature. Partly as a legacy of the Roman dramatist Seneca, a husband betrayed by his wife, a father whose son, or a son whose father, had been murdered, has the duty of taking vengeance on the wrongdoer. In different ways Kyd's *Spanish Tragedy*, Chapman's *The Revenge of Bussy D'Ambois* and *Hamlet* belong to this type though the avengers delay in carrying out their mission. It was therefore a revolution against theatrical precedent to represent the injured parties intent not on vengeance but mercy and forgiveness. In Jane's case there are two, her husband and Edward's queen. In a touching if over-sentimental scene, unique of its kind, the Queen, though urged by her son to take revenge, raises Jane who is kneeling at her feet and pleads with her :

O God forbid that Edward's queen should hate
Her, whom she knows he doth so dearly love.
My love to her may purchase me his love,

*   *   *   *   *   *

Thou art my sister, and I love thee so.
I know thou mayest do much with my dear lord.

Jane. All I can do is all too little too
      But to requite the least part of this grace.

But with Edward's death, and Richard's installation as Lord Protector, Jane is thrust forth to walk the streets in a white sheet, barefooted and in her hand a burning taper. When all turn from her, it is her husband who takes her dying into his arms.

Jane. Ah, Shore, is't possible thou can'st forgive
      me ?
Shore. Yes, Jane I do.
Jane. I cannot hope thou wilt.
      My fault's so great that I cannot expect it.
Shore. I'faith I do, as freely from my soul,
      As at God's hands I hope to be forgiven.

The part of Jane Shore must have been an exacting one for a boy actor in Lord Derby's company. His youthful colleagues doubtless found it easier to impersonate the two young princes in the Tower, filled with foreboding but kneeling to say their prayers before they go to the beds from which they are never to rise alive.

It is to be noted that a popular comic figure in the play Hobs, the Tanner of Tamworth, asks the King, " Dost thou not know me ? " and when the answer is " no," retorts " Then thou knowest nobody ! " It is this proverbial phrase, which gives its first title irrelevantly, to another two part play of which the first part is more truly called by its second title, *The Troubles of Queen Elizabeth.* This too was published anonymously by Nathaniel Butter in 1605, but is known to be Heywood's by his inclusion of his prologue to a revival of it at the Cockpit Theatre about 1623, in his miscellany of *Pleasant Dialogues and Dramas.* This prologue contains the classical reference to the pirating of plays by shorthand. Heywood complains that some by stenography drew

> The plot : put it in print (scarce one word trew)
> And in that lameness it hath limpt so long
> The author now to vindicate that wrong,
> Hath took the pains, upright upon its feet
> To teach it walk, so please you sit, and see't.

The text printed by Butter of Part I to which Heywood here refers does indeed limp for it is very much shorter than that of the average play of the period and is padded out with three dumb shows. But it is astonishing that no less than six further editions of it appeared up to 1639 without any amendment, and indeed with all its imperfections Part I presents an

attractive and lively picture of Elizabeth in her troubles
during the reign of her sister.* When Gardiner, the
Bishop of Winchester, and the Constable of the Tower,
where she is for a time immured, try to prove her guilty
of treason she scornfully rejects the charge :

> Treason, Lords ! If it be treason
> To be the daughter to th' eighth Henry,
> Sister to Edward, and the next of blood
> Unto my gracious sovereign, the now Queen,
> I am a traitor : if not, I spit at treason.

When the Constable retorts :

> Madam, The Queen must hear you sing another
>   song,
> Before you part with us :

Elizabeth answers :

> My God doth know
> I can no note but truth ; that with Heaven's King
> One day in quires of angels I shall sing.
> *Winch.* Then, madam, you will not submit ?
> *Eliz.* My life, I will, but not as guilty.

On the other hand the persecuted girl finds compas-
sionate friends, especially in the Earl of Sussex and
King Philip. It is characteristic of Heywood's tolerant
sympathies that on the one side he shows the Roman
Catholic sovereign interceding with Queen Mary to
" look on your sister with a tolerant brow," and on
the other, after Mary's death and Elizabeth's accession,
he presents the Lord Mayor offering the new queen a

*I have dealt more fully with this play in an essay on " Queen
Elizabeth in English Drama " in a volume recently published by
Allen & Unwin.

Bible which she welcomes with a kiss and a fervently joyous acclamation :

> An English Bible ! Thanks, my good Lord Mayor,
> You of our body and our soul have care
> This is the jewel that we still love best ;
> This was our solace, when we were distrest,
> This book that hath so long concealed itself,
> So long shut up, so long hid, now lords, see,
> We here unclasp : for ever it is free.*

The historical episodes dramatised by Heywood in Part I were retold by him in prose in the later pages of *England's Elizabeth her life and troubles during her minority, from the Cradle to the Crown* (1631). The earlier part of this volume, taken mainly from Holinshed, Fabyan and Foxe, dealt with the fall of Anne Boleyn and the reign of Lady Jane Grey. Dr. Clark has suggested that these may have already been dramatised in the lost play *Lady Jane* for which Heywood, with four collaborators, was paid by Henslowe in October, 1602.

Part II of *If you Know not me, you Know Nobody* with its sub-title, *With the Building of the Royal Exchange and the famous Victory of Queen Elizabeth. Anno 1588*, was also published anonymously by N. Butter in 1606. It was reprinted in 1609, 1623, and 1632, with the closing Armada episode amplified in the last edition. The text is in much better presentation than in Part I, but Elizabeth is not the central figure. This place is filled

---

*The translation by Tindale and Coverdale, the so-called Matthews Bible, and the Great Bible, of which there were seven editions between 1539–41, had considerable circulation before Mary's reign, but during it no English Bibles were printed, and many were destroyed. In 1560 the Genevan Bible was the work of a number of Protestant Refugees. This was followed in 1568 by the Bishops' Bible, of which there were later editions. Elizabeth allowed any form of Bible to be used, provided there was one in every parish church and every M.A. had a New Testament.

by the wealthy merchant, Thomas Gresham, through whose lips and actions Heywood again finds a vent for his civic patriotism. Inspired by pictures of former London worthies, shown to him by the Dean of St. Paul's, including Lord Mayor Walworth, already mentioned in *Edward IV* and Richard Whittington, and driven to take shelter from a sudden storm, Gresham determines to build a great " Burse " or Exchange where,

> It shall be in the pleasure of my life
> To come and meet our merchants at their hour,
> And see them in the greatest storm that is
> Walk dry and in a work I rais'd for them.

When it is completed the Russian ambassador visits the Burse and is welcomed through an interpreter in Latin. The ambassador asks :

> What interpreter the Queen
> Would in his embassy employ,

to which Gresham replies :

> None, tell him none,
> For though a woman she is a rare linguist,
> She of herself answers them without interpreter,
> Both Spanish, Latin, French and Greek,
> Dutch and Italian, so let him know.

She is soon after, on a visit to the City, shown on the stage talking in their own tongues with the French and Florentine ambassadors, before proceeding to give a name to the new Burse. Calling for a herald and a trumpet she commands :

> Proclaim through every high street of this city
> This place to be no longer called a Burse,

> But since the building's stately fair and strange,
> Be it for ever call'd the Royal Exchange :
> And whiles this voice flies through the City forthright,
> Arise, Sir Thomas Gresham, now a Knight.

There are some features of Heywood's earlier and cruder portraiture, as when Gresham dances in the slippers sent by a King of Barbary in repudiating a contract which costs the merchant £60,000 ; and when he has a pearl priced £1,500 beaten to powder in a cup of wine which he drinks to the queen's health.

> Who ever saw a merchant bravelier fraught
> In dearer slippers, or a richer draught ?

Yet in spite of these extravagances Gresham stands out as a true " royal merchant," and he has his patriotic counterpart in a humbler civic grade in old Hobson, a haberdasher, who when the queen sends to borrow £100 from him presses double the sum upon her messenger. It is he who later speaks to her the words which give the play its title.

Hobson. God bless thy grace, Queen Bess.
Eliz. Friend, what art thou ?
Hobson. Knowest thou not me, Queen ; then thou
knowest nobody !
Bones-a-me, Queen, I am Hobson.

Together with his apprentices and a customer known as " Tawneycoat " and Gresham's scapegrace nephew, Jack, he supplies the too long drawn out comic relief. The close is supplied by history with the irrelevant episode of Parry's attempt on Elizabeth's life, and the defeat of the Armada, related in turn by posts, a captain and Sir Francis Drake, and considerably amplified in the 1632 edition.

We have to turn back to the reign of Elizabeth's father for an almost certain small but interesting addition to the Heywood canon made only by recent criticism. The MS. *Harl. 7368* in the British Museum, *Sir Thomas More*, is in various hands of which those of Munday, Chettle, and Dekker have been identified and another (D) has been authoritatively claimed as that of Shakespeare. It was Dr. Greg who first pointed out the resemblance of the atrocious hand (B) in the MS. to that of plays by Heywood in another B.M. MS. *Egerton 1994*, and Heywood's authorship of the " B " additions has been widely accepted on palaeographical grounds. I may add that it would be an attraction to Heywood that the earlier half of the play is concerned with incidents in London civic life. The two chief contributions in his hand are f. 7ª and f. 16. The former is an elaboration of a scene in the anti-alien rising of the Londoners on the " ill " Mayday of 1517. The second is an addition of sixty-seven lines to the original script, a supplement to the scene in which Sir Thomas More as Sheriff presents an interlude in his house before the Lord Mayor and Mayoress.

CHAPTER 2

ADVENTURE PLAYS

The Four Prentices of London—The Fair Maid of the West, Parts I and II.

If Sir E. K. Chambers is right in his suggestion that the safest guess about the date of *Sir Thomas More* is 1596, Heywood's contribution to this composite play was made probably a few years before he wrote *The Four Prentices of London : With the Conquest of Jerusalem*, first published in 1615, but stated in his apologetic prefatory epistle to have been written some fifteen or sixteen years ago, " in my infancy of judgment in this kind of Poetry and my first practice." His excuse is that unknown to him it had come to the press in such forwardness that it was past prevention, and that its publication coincided with a striking signal of civic patriotism, the revival of the " commendable practice of long forgotten arms " in the Artillery Garden. The technique of the play is indeed immature, with its sprawling action and its use of a presenter and a dumb show and except for " Actus primus, Scaena prima " no indication of Act or Scene divisions. Yet it claims attention for it combines further sketches of city life with other features which were to reappear in Heywood's plays, romantic adventures by sea and land and pseudo-history.

The Earl of Boulogne, a supporter of William of Normandy in his conquest of England, has been dispossessed by the French King and is living in London as a citizen, with his four sons apprenticed to different trades. About to make a pilgrimage to the Holy Land he asks them how they like their different lots. Godfrey, the senior, answers cheerfully,

> I praise that City that made princes tradesmen,
>
>   *   *   *   *   *
>
> I hold it no disparage to my birth,
> Though I be born an Earl to have the skill
> And the full knowledge of the Mercer's trade.

The second son Guy, more reservedly calls the Goldsmith's faculty " a good refuge in extremity " and Charles, the third, a Haberdashee chimes in :

> As my two brothers, I reply,
> You ask me if I like it, I say " Aye."

Eustace, the youngest, a grocer, is restive under a severe master.

> He will not let me see a mustering,
> Nor on a May-day morning fetch in May :
> I am no sooner got into the fencing school
> To play a venue with some friend I bring,
> But, " Eustace, Eustace " all the street must ring.
> He will allow me not one hour for sport.
> I must not strike a football in the street
> But he will frown, not view the dancing school
> But he will miss me straight ; not suffer me
> So much as take up cudgels in the street
> But he will chide.

Could there be a more lively picture of the recreations of a young high-spirited Elizabethan prentice, varied in details but in essentials the same of his opposite number today ? Had all the play been on this level

Heywood would not have needed to make any apology for its shortcomings.

At the sound of a drum, and of a summons to all who will to follow the Conqueror's eldest son Robert on a crusade to Jerusalem, the brothers at once respond, with Eustace characteristically giving the lead ! " I'll home no more, I'll run away tonight."

Guy, the goldsmith, follows suit :

> If I cast bowl, or spoon, or salt again,
> Before I have beheld Jerusalem,
> Let me turn pagan.

So too Charles, the haberdasher,

> Hats and caps adieu,
> For I must leave you if the drums say true.

Even the more restrained Godfrey, the mercer, also catches the infection.

> Give me your hands : I will consort you too.
> Let's try what London prentices can do.

They agree to carry the arms of their various trades in their ensigns—a feature which Beaumont was to turn to ridicule in his play *The Knight of the Burning Pestle*.

Then there succeeds a series of wildly erratic episodes, with a sentimental addition supplied by Bella Franca who has followed her four brothers to the Crusade and becomes the bride of the Italian prince Tancred, and by the French King's daughter in whom Guy finds a mate.

With the arrival of the Crusaders before Jerusalem Heywood's truly reverential spirit raises the scene to an impressive level. The speeches of the war-leaders before the walls form a sort of chant with a refrain :

Duke Robert.   O Princes, which of all your eyes are
dry,
To look upon this Temple, now destroy'd ? . . .
Now in that holy place, where God
himself
Was personally present, Pagans dwell,
False gods are rear'd, each temple idols
bears.
O who can see this and abstain from
tears ?

Godfrey.   Within this place did stand the judg-
ment seat
Where Pontius Pilate with the elders sat,
Where they condemn'd him to be
whipt and crown'd,
To be derided, mocked and crucified,
His hands bor'd through with nails,
his side with spears.
O who can see this place and keep his
tears ?

Charles.   There stood the Cross, there stands the
Sepulchre,
The place still bears the name of *Dead
Men's Bones*
And still the Tomb our Saviour's livery
wears.
What eye can see it and not melt in
tears ?

Tar.   No soldier but shall look with reverence
Upon these fair and glorious monu-
ments,
To swear, or speak profanely, shall be
death.
O since our wars are God's, abandon
fears,
But in contrition weep repentant tears.

It is something of a lyrical *tour de force* with its skilful variation of rhymes in the concluding couplets.

There is more of a dramatic element in the contrast between the two pagan chiefs, the Soldan of Babylon who seeks at first a policy of appeasement with the Christians, if they come as pilgrims, and the younger Sophy of Persia, who, with a more realistic instinct, is for immediate war. When, after the battle-scenes beloved by an Elizabethan audience, the Crusaders are victorious, it is natural that the old Earl should be invested as Patriarch of Jerusalem, but it is a *coup de théâtre* that Godfrey should choose instead of a preferred Crown, one of thorns, while his brother Guy becomes King of Jerusalem, Eustace of Sicily and Charles of Cyprus, each hanging up his scutcheon with the blazon of his trade.

The combination in *The Four Prentices* of domestic scenes, romantic adventure and a historical background reappears at a considerably later date in Heywood's dramatic activity and in a much maturer form in the two-part play, *The Fair Maid of the West, or A Girl Worth Gold*, published in 1631, " as it was lately acted before the King and Queen, with approved liking by the Queen's Majesty's Comedians, written by T.H." As the Prologue and Epilogue were spoken before their two Majesties at Hampton Court, this performance evidently took place there. But Part I of *The Fair Maid of the West*, which in itself is a complete play, was probably originally acted much earlier when the stirring event which forms the background of the opening scene was still comparatively fresh in popular memory.

Two Captains at Plymouth are preparing to set sail among a gallant company under the Earl of Essex in 1597 on what was to be known as the " island voyage "

to do battle for their treasure fleet with the Spaniards.
They had been heartened by Drake's exploits, and are
now all on fire

> To purchase from the Spaniard. If their carracks
> Come deeply laden, we shall try with them
> For golden spoil.

One of the Captains cries enthusiastically " O will it
come to that ? " and the other replies :

> How Plymouth swells with gallants ; how the streets
> Glisten with gold ! You cannot meet a man
> But tricked in scarf and feather, that it seems
> As if the pride of England's gallantry
> Were harboured here. It doth appear, methinks,
> A very court of soldiers.

Among the gallants is Captain Spencer, a gentleman
of fortune who is taking part in this voyage not, as
many others, in the hope of gain or spoil but for honour.
Meanwhile he has become enamoured of the fair maid
of the west, below him in birth and breeding, Bess
Bridges, daughter of a trade-fallen Somerset tanner,
who has sent her to serve as a tavern wench in Plymouth. To save her from insult in a tavern-quarrel
Spencer kills a man called Carrol, and has to set out at
once. But before sailing he bestows on Bess his trunks
and their contents, his

> Picture which in my chamber hangs,
> For when thou part'st with that, thou losest me,

and a tavern that he owns in Foy in Cornwall, to which
he will send news of himself. As he is about to take

his leave Bess cries in words that would befit Juliet's
lips :

> O that I had the power to make Time lame,
> To stay the stars, or make the moon stand still,
> That future day might never haste thy flight.
> I could dwell here for ever in thine arms,
> And wish it always night.

She then hands him the ring which was the first token
of their mutual love, declaring that when she next sees
it, and not him, she will think him dead. The next
scene, it is of interest to notice, is a dumb show, in
which Essex, on the point of departure appears with
the Captains and the Mayors, and gives bags of money
to the tavern drawers to discharge his account. The
tradition of Essex as a free-handed leader of men
evidently survived.

The scene shifts to the Windmill in Foy, where in
Heywood's happiest lighter vein Bess is seen standing
up to the swaggerer Ruffman and casting up accounts
with the sharp-witted apprentice Clem. Then there
is an overseas shift to Fayal in the Azores where Spencer
intervening, like Romeo, in a fray between the two
Captains is wounded, as he thinks to death, by one of
them, also called Spencer. Thinking himself bound upon a new adventure to the other world, he commissions
his friend Goodlack to convey to Bess at Foy a legacy
of £500 a year, on condition that there is no scandal on
her name, in which case Goodlack himself is to be
inheritor. Her picture of him is also to be taken away,
if she has proved false, but her ring, as it is her own, is
to be restored.

An Atlantic breeze blows through the theatre as a
sailor enters shouting,

Aboard Aboard ! the wind stands fair for England.
The ships have all weighed anchor . . .
Sir, will you take the long-boat and aboard ?

As Goodlack follows the sailor, a bell tolls to announce
a death, and another sailor shouts,

They say 'twas for one Spencer, who this night
Died of a mortal wound.

Goodlack takes it to be his friend, but it is the other
Spencer who had been wounded during the fray. Here
Heywood stretches the long arm of coincidence too far ;
it is the weakest point in the technique of the play.
Spencer himself recovers, and the surgeon who has
attended him offers him a free passage in his ship now
bound for Marmorah in Barbary but due to return to
England ten months hence.

When Goodlack reaches Foy he finds that Bess has
an untarnished reputation, but in order to get the an-
nuity for himself, he tries to blacken her fame by calling
her whore and harlot, and provoke her to fury by declaring that Spencer with his last breath had bidden
him deface his picture. As she implores him to let her
at least take her leave of it, she speaks to it in exquisitely
touching terms :

O thou, the perfect semblance of my love,
And all that's left of him, take one sweet kiss
At my last farewell ! Thou resemblest him
For whose sweet safety I was every morning
Down on my knees, and with the lark's sweet tunes
I did begin my prayers ; and when sad sleep
Had charmed all eyes, when none save the bright
   stars
Were up and waking, I remembered thee,
But all, all to no purpose.

Her devotion at last overpowers Goodlack and he not only restores the picture, but gives her the ring, and the written proofs of the legacy.

Then follows a series of romantic adventures which, in more artistic form, spring from the same impulse that gave birth to the oriental elements in *The Four Prentices of London*. Bess makes use of Spencer's legacy to fit out a ship of which in man's disguise she will have chief command with Goodlack as captain and Ruffman, converted to better ways, as lieutenant. Its destination is Fayal to bring back what she thinks to be her Spencer's body, but from a captured Spanish prisoner she learns that the body (really not of her Spencer) had been treated with indignity, as that of a heretic, and burnt.

Meanwhile the ship in which the real Spencer of her search was sailing to Barbary had been captured by the Spaniards, who show their usual brutality and insolence to their English prisoners. But in its turn the Spanish ship is taken by Bess and her crew, Goodlack is wounded and has to retire to his cabin. Thus he is not at hand to recognise Spencer when with the other English prisoners he comes aboard Bess's ship. She almost faints at the sight, taking him for a ghost.

Is it because the Spaniards scaped with life,
That were to thee so cruel after death,
Thou haunt'st me thus, sweet ghost, thy rage forbear,
I will revenge thee on the next we seize.

Spencer does not recognise her in her male disguise though he sees a resemblance to his beloved Bess. Throughout these scenes Heywood unlike his attitude towards Philip in Part I of *If You Know not Me, You*

Know Nobody, makes a strong appeal to the patriotic
and anti-Spanish feeling of his audience.

Before Act V, like Shakespeare in *Henry V*, he has to
piece out his dramatic technique with a chorus—As he
frankly declares :

> Our stage so lamely can express a sea
> That we are forced by Chorus to express
> What should have been in action.

The Chorus tell that Bess after taking many prizes at
sea had been forced by want to put into Marmorah in
Barbary where Spencer's ship had already arrived. She
had changed into feminine garb and Moors coming
aboard had reported her beauty to King Mullisheg.
When she lands he at once becomes enamoured of her
and declares :

> This is no mortal creature I behold,
> But some bright angel that is dropped from Heaven,
> Sent by our prophet.

When he hears that her name is Elizabeth, he exclaims :

> There's virtue in that name.
> The Virgin queen so famous through the
> world
> Is not she titled so ? *Bess.* She is.
> *Mull.* Hath she herself a face so fair as yours ?
> *Bess.* You cast a blush upon my maiden cheek
> To pattern me with her. Why, England's
> queen,
> She is the only phoenix of her age,
> The pride and glory of the Western Isles.

This is an unexpected tribute to Queen Elizabeth by
an African monarch. It is really another recognition by
Heywood of the greatness of the queen whose earlier

years had been the theme of his *If You Know not Me, You Know Nobody*.

The King invites Bess to share his royal seat, and at her plea shows clemency to various offenders, including the master of the ship which had brought Spencer to Barbary. When Spencer himself appears Bess again takes him for a ghost, but Goodlack, now by her side, recognises him and the King, showing himself truly magnanimous, conquers his own passion and unites her, as " a precedent of all true love " to her faithful wooer.

Heywood was ill advised in adding a Part II to one of his most attractive and accomplished pieces of work. By an incredible transformation the hitherto high-minded King, together with his queen Tota, have lustful designs on Bess and Spencer but are tricked into each other's arms by night. It is only by a competition in self-sacrifice of Spencer, Bess, Goodlack and Ruffman, and a Moorish Bashaw that the King at the end of Act III is moved to grant life and liberty to them all. With the aid again of a chorus and a dumb-show prefixed to Act IV Bess and Spencer are parted on their homeward voyage during a fight with pirates, and Bess has to suffer the amorous advances of three Italian Dukes, and an apparent repulse by her husband, before all ends happily.

CHAPTER 3

Collaboration for Henslowe—Domestic Dramas
A Woman Killed with Kindness—The English Traveller

It has been conjectured that there is a reference to the
Four Prentices in an entry by Henslowe on 3rd September, 1602, " Layd owt for the company to bye iiij lances
for the comody of thomas hewedes and mr. smythes,
some of viijs," with a further entry on the following
day of a " thinge for thomas heywode playe." Mr.
Smith was Wentworth Smith who collaborated in a
number of lost plays during 1601–3 for Henslowe's
Companies, and whose *Hector of Germany* was published
in 1615. But the reference to the *Four Prentices* is doubtful and Heywood's preface does not speak of any hand
in the play but his own. He and Smith were to have
further collaboration for Henslowe paid them £6 for
a play which he calls *albere galles*, a title which has defied
identification, though I think that the most plausible
guess is that it is a corruption of Archigallo, a character
in a popular play *Nobody and Somebody* (S.R. 12th March,
1605–6), apparently a revision of an older piece. His
next payment was £1 for additions to a play called
Cutting Dick, the hero of which was Dick Evans, a
notable highwayman in Wiltshire who in December
1601 was taken and like to be hanged.

Further payments were made to Smith and Heywood
for a play *Marshal Osric* and to them with Chettle,
Dekker and Webster for *Lady Jane*, £8 among the five.
The play is lost, but Dekker's and Webster's contributions are generally supposed to survive in *The Famous*

[37]

History of Sir Thomas Wyatt, and Dr. Clark has suggested that Heywood's share is preserved in *If You Know not Me, You Know Nobody*, Part I and some scenes of Part II. The dramatists of *Lady Jane*, except Smith, next collaborated in November on *Christmas comes but once a year*, probably a play for the holiday season ; and in three instalments between 24th November, 1602 and 7th January, 1602–3 Heywood received £6 for a piece with the odd name, *The Blind eats many a fly*.

Little is known of Heywood's domestic life during this journeyman period of his career. It has been assumed while he was acting at the Rose that he lived on the Bankside, and that when Queen Anne's men migrated to the Curtain he would cross the river to Clerkenwell where he had a residence near Clerkenwell Hill. Dr. Clark has found in the register of St. Antholin's Church, an entry, 13th June, 1603 " Thomas Hayward was married to Aenn Butler, serv^t to Mr. Venn ? " If this was the dramatist, we would have expected a union with someone of rather higher social status. At least six children were born of the marriage. Dr. Clark gives a list of some of the more notable Clerkenwell residents with whom there is evidence of different kinds that he was connected. And he must have had many friends among his fellow-players to whom in his *Apology for Actors* he pays so notable a tribute.

As we are men that stand in the broad eye of the world, so should our manners, gestures, behaviours savour of such government and modesty, to deserve the good thoughts and reports of all men. Many among us I know to be of substance, of government, of sober lives, and temperate carriages, housekeepers, and contributory to all duties enjoined them.

What a contrast is this from one speaking from inside with intimate knowledge of his fellow professionals to the Oxonian Gager's description of actors as "of a lewd, vast, dissolute, wicked, impudent, prodigal, monstrous humour," or to the Cambridge author of *The Return from Parnassus* deriding them as vagabonds,

> Sooping it in their glaring satin suits,
> And pages to attend their masterships.

If our Thomas Heywood was the bridegroom of Anne Butler in June, 1603, she was just in time to share his rejoicing in the triumph of *A Woman Killed with Kindness*, which was to set the seal on his reputation as a dramatist.

In dealing with the *Jane Shore* scenes in *King Edward IV* I drew attention to the fact that Heywood, in Shore's merciful treatment of his erring wife, was reversing the tradition of the Elizabethan revenge plays. He was to present, in far more artistic fashion, another example of the tenderly forgiving husband in the most moving of all his plays, *A Woman Killed with Kindness*. Henslowe records in his *Diary* that he paid Heywood £3 for the play on 12th February, 1602–3, followed by another £3 on 6th March. He had already on 5th February paid £7 15s. od. for a woman's gown of black velvet for the play, and on 7th March he added 10s. od. to the tailor who made a black satin suit for it. It was more profitable to provide costumes for the play than to be its author.

Heywood now transports his audience from London where (except for the expedition to Palestine) the scenes of the plays hitherto discussed have been laid, to a country house in Yorkshire. The wedding of Master Frankford with Nan Acton has just been

celebrated and relatives and friends are showering
their congratulations, led by Sir Charles Mountford.

> Master Frankford,
> You are a happy man, sir, and much joy,
> Succeed your marriage mirth ! You have a wife
> So qualified, and with such ornaments,
> Both of the mind and body . . .
> To end her many praises in one word,
> She's beauty and perfection's eldest daughter,
> Only found by yours, though many a heart hath
>   sought her.

And after others, including the bride's brother, Sir
Francis Acton, have chimed in, Sir Charles continues.

> You are both
> Scholars, both young, both being descended nobly,
> There's music in this sympathy, it carries,
> Consort, and expectation of much joy,
> Which God bestow on you, from this first day
> Until your dissolution : that's for aye !

In these last words there is a challenge to fortune
which is to have a mockingly inimical answer.
At the beginning of Act II Frankford is still rejoicing
in " the chief of all the sweet felicities on earth."

> I have a fair, a chaste and loving wife,
> Perfection all, all truth, all ornament,
> If man on earth may truly happy be,
> Of these at once possessed, sure I am he.

But he has taken into his house, to use his table and
purse as his own, a gentleman of poor means, Master
Wendoll, who, after a struggle with his conscience while
Frankford is absent, declares his passion for Nan. She
yields to this dependant of her husband more quickly

than Jane Shore to her King, though her cheek bears
witness to her guilt.

> I blush and am ashamed, Oh, Master Wendoll,
> Pray God I be not born to curse your tongue,
> That hath enchanted me ! This maze I am in
> I fear will prove the labyrinth of sin.

The faithful old servant, Nicholas, reveals their guilt
to Frankford on his return, but cannot convince him,
though there runs an undercurrent of his suspicion in
his remarks during a game of cards, which shows
Heywood's familiarity with many varieties of card-
games, and throws light on their history in Elizabethan
times.

Mrs. Frank.	Husband, shall we play at Saint ?*
Frank.	My saint's turned devil. No we'll none of saint.
	You are best at new-cut,* wife, you'll play at that.
Wend.	If you play at new-cut, I am soonest hither Of any here, for a wager.
Frank.	'Tis me they play on. Well, you may draw out.
	For all your cunning, 'twill be to your shame.
	I'll teach you, at your new-cut, a new game.

Suspicion turns to certainty when Frankford finds them
lying, " Close in each other's arms and fast asleep."
His religious scruples prevent him from taking summary
vengeance on the guilty pair.

> But that I would not damn two precious souls,
> Bought with my Saviour's blood, and send them laden
> With all their scarlet sins upon their backs
> Unto a fearful judgment, their two lives
> Had met upon my rapier.

* Card games.

And the wish, the inevitable but vain wish, that the past could be undone has never found more poignant utterance than from Frankford's lips :

O God ! O God ! that it were possible
To undo things done, to call back yesterday !
That Time could turn up his swift sandy glass,
To untell the days and to redeem these hours !
Or that the sun
Could rising from the west, draw his coach backward,
Take from the account of time so many minutes,
Till he had all these seasons called again,
Those minutes, and those actions done in them,
Even from her first offence : that I might take her
As spotless as an angel in my arms !
But oh ! I talk of things impossible,
And cast beyond the moon.

Nan's repentance is as sudden as had been her sin. As she kneels at Frankford's feet she sobs.

O by what word, what title, or what name,
Shall I entreat your pardon ? Pardon ! oh,
I am as far from hoping such sweet grace
As Lucifer from heaven. To call you husband—
O me most wretched ! I have lost that name,
I am no more your wife.

And Heywood shows himself master of a subtle psychological touch when he makes the angered husband declare that it is he who has most cause for shame.

Spare thou thy tears, for I will weep for thee ;
And keep thy countenance, for I'll blush for thee.
Now, I protest, I think 'tis I am tainted,
For I am most ashamed.

Nan is prepared for any punishment, even death, but her husband's decree is that she is to retire with full equipment and service to his manor seven miles off. She cries, " A mild sentence ! " but there is more

to follow. She is never to see or have communication
with him or their children. It is an equivocal form of
" Kindness," which kills Nan as surely as a sword, for
she will not have food or drink or sleep, and is on her
deathbed when her husband breaks his own pro-
nouncement and comes to her side. Again she begs
forgiveness from him whom she dare not call husband.

> O good man,
> And father of my children, pardon me !
> Pardon, oh pardon me ! My fault so heinous is
> That if you in this world forgive it not,
> Heaven will not clear it in the world to come.

To my mind there is no nobler passage in Elizabethan
drama than Frankford's answer :

> As freely from the low depth of my soul,
> As my Redeemer hath forgiven His death,
> I pardon thee. I will shed tears for thee,
> Pray with thee and in mere pity
> Of thy weak state I'll wish to die with thee.

For a moment, and it is a deft dramatic touch, Nicholas,
the old retainer, breaks the solemnity of the scene by
murmuring,

> So will not I.
> I'll sigh and sob, but, by my faith, not die.

It is not only forgiveness but reunion that Frankford
proclaims :

> Even as I hope for pardon at that day
> When the great Judge of Heaven in scarlet sits,
> So be thou pardoned. Though thy rash offence
> Divorced our bodies, thy repentant tears
> Unite our souls . . .
> My wife, the mother to my pretty babes,
> Both those last names I do restore thee back,
> And with this kiss I wed thee once again.

I wonder what was the reaction of the gallants and groundlings in the theatre of Heywood's day, who in that very year 1603 were to see, though imperfectly, the greatest of "revenge" tragedies *Hamlet* in book form, to this sacred scene of reconciliation. But I know how deeply it moved a modern dramatist, John Drinkwater, beside whom I sat at the Malvern Festival revival of the play.

Very loosely connected with the main theme is an underplot in which Nan's brother, Sir Francis Acton, after a situation in some ways akin to that of Claudio and Isabella in *Measure for Measure*, becomes united to Susan Mountford, a paragon of sisterly devotion.

The maturity of Heywood's work in *A Woman Killed with Kindness* compared with any of the plays which we can assign to him previously is remarkable. Its success was immediate. In Middleton's pamphlet, *The Black Book* (1604) a young fellow is given leave to see either it or *The Merry Devil of Edmonton*. In 1607 an edition appeared, the first of Heywood's plays bearing his name ; printed by William Jaggard and sold by John Hodgets. Of this only one surviving copy in the British Museum is recorded by the Short Title Catalogue. The second edition has completely disappeared, of a third edition for Isaac Jaggard, 1617, there are a good many copies.

Dates are of less importance in Heywood's case than with some of his contemporaries, and it will be convenient to skip over some years and turn to *The English Traveller*, printed in 1633, but probably publicly acted by the Queen's Company at the Cockpit, some years earlier. In this play Heywood, presents a remarkable and enigmatic variant to the theme of *A Woman Killed with Kindness*. He was now dramatising a story which

he had already related in prose in his Γυναικειον
(1624). In that collecton of " Various History concerning Women," as will be seen more fully later,
Heywood exemplified many of his general comments
by short stories. One of the most detailed of these is
related in the section of Book IV dealing with adulteresses. Heywood expressly states that it is " a modern
history, lately happening, and in mine own knowledge."
It is probably on this account that he gives no names
to the characters but designates them as an " elderly
gentleman " married to " a beautiful and well-bred
young gentlewoman," and in close friendship with
" the son of a neighbour who had travelled far and
wide," and who had a " best friend." In turning the
story into a play Heywood had to give (doubtless
fictitious) names to the characters, but otherwise he
stuck close to the details of his prose narrative. The
English Traveller is young Geraldine, just returned
after a long absence that has taken him as far as
Jerusalem. He finds that his elderly neighbour, Wincott,
has married his own former young playfellow and
sweetheart, whose name is never given, unlike that of
her lively sister, Prudentilla. Wincott welcomes
Geraldine to his home in words that recall Frankford's
invitation to Wendoll :

> I would have you
> Think this your home, free as your father's house,
> And to command it, as the master on't.
> Call boldly here, and entertain your friends
> As in your own possessions : When I see't
> I'll say you love me truly, not till then.

Mistress Wincott tells Geraldine that her husband loves
to hear his tales of his travels. But these are not of

" antres strange and deserts wild," with which Othello fascinated Desdemona. Again Heywood shows, as in *The Four Prentices*, his keen interest in Jerusalem and the Holy Land :

> How the new city differs from the old,
> What ruins of the temple yet remain,
> And whether Sion, and those hills about,
> With the adjacent towns and villages,
> Keep that proportioned distance, as we read.

The other main topic of Geraldine's discourse is Rome,

> How many of those idol temples stand,
> First dedicated to their heathen gods,
> Which ruined, which to better use repaired :
> Of their Pantheon and their Capitol—
> What structures are demolished, what remain.

Geraldine and the wife do not abuse Wincott's trust, but they vow that when in nature's course the old man dies they will wed. All would be well had not Geraldine's false friend, with the suggestive name of Delavil, while playing like Iago on the word " honest," insinuated into the mind of Geraldine's father the suspicion that his son is guilty of misconduct with Mistress Wincott. To clear himself the father insists that Geraldine must forbear the house where he has been so constant and welcome a guest. Delavil takes advantage of his absence to win the favours of the wife, and even more than in *A Woman Killed with Kindness* this is the weakest point in Heywood's technique, for Mistress Wincott falls from virtue even without the short struggle of Nan Frankford and though she is doubly pledged to her husband and Geraldine.

A chambermaid reveals this to Geraldine and he thus

feels free, in spite of his father's decree, to comply with
Wincott's urgent appeal by letter that he should re-
visit their house privately by night. He finds the guilty
pair in each other's arms. For a moment like Frankford
he thinks of instant vengeance.

> Out my sword !
> I'll act a noble execution
> On two unmatched for sordid villainy—.
> I left it in my chamber, and thank Heaven
> That I did so . . . I once loved her,
> And was to her entire. Although I pardon,
> Heaven will find time to punish.

Unlike Nan Frankford and her lover Mistress Wincott
and Delavil do not know that they have been dis-
covered together, and when Geraldine announces that
he will set out again on his travels, she hypocritically
begs him to stay for her sake :—

> Why will you travel, suing a divorce
> Betwixt us of a love inseparable ;
> For here shall I be left as desolate
> Unto a frozen, almost widowed bed
> Oh, sir, should you miscarry, I were lost,
> Lost and forsaken. Then by our past vows
> I do beseech thee, my dear Geraldine,
> Look to thy safety and preserve thy health . . .
> For till Heavens bless me in thy safe return
> How will this poor heart suffer !

Then at last Geraldine, who, " so fixed was his love
and unalterable," has kept her sin secret from her
husband, turns upon her, and bids her

> Die and die soon ; acquit me of my oath,
> But prithee, die repentant

She sinks in a swoon and is carried out to die, but not till she has made confession to her husband :

Delavil
Hath played the villan, but for Geraldine,
He hath been each way noble : love him still,
My peace already I have made with Heaven.

And in the spirit of Frankford, Wincott declares, " Where Heaven forgives, I pardon ! " But we are left with the feeling that his wife's misconduct has been much less agonising to him than to Geraldine, and her sudden demise and confidence that she has made all right with Heaven cannot move us like the long drawn-out pathos of Nan Frankford's death-bed scene. Yet Heywood's variations on the theme of the erring and forgiven wife in Jane Shore, Nan, and Mistress Wincott are of special interest to all students of his technique.

CHAPTER 4

Plays from Classical Sources—Edition of Marlowe's "Jew of Malta"

With the main theme of *The English Traveller* was loosely connected, in Heywood's characteristic fashion, a sub-plot borrowed from a classical source, the *Mostellaria*, or *Ghost-story*, of Plautus. A young man Lionel, during his father's absence on a sea voyage keeps revel with dissipated companions of both sexes, who, in the words of Robin, an honest country servant,

Keep Christmas all year long, and blot lean Lent
Out of the calendar.

The climax of their riotous merry-making is when they pretend that the room in which they are feasting is a ship storm-tossed at sea, and to save their lives cast the lading overboard :

Stools, tables, trestles, trenchers, bedsteads, cups,
Pots, plate and glasses,

for which the crowd outside go to fisticuffs. The account of this is an admirable piece of humorous narrative. Suddenly Lionel's father enters and, to keep him out of the house, Reginald, a crafty servant familiar in Roman comedy, hoaxes him into the belief that the house is haunted by the ghost of a man murdered there by the former owner of the house. The further complications and their solutions are skilfully worked out.

Another debt of Heywood to Plautus was not recognised till some sixty years ago. Among the plays in the

British Museum MS. volume *Egerton 1994*, there is one, *The Captives, or The Lost Recovered*. This was identified by A. H. Bullen as being in Heywood's peculiarly difficult handwriting, and was first printed by him in Volume IV of his *Old English Plays* (1885). It has since been edited, with a more detailed apparatus of introduction and notes, by A. C. Judson (1921). It was entered by the Master of the Revels, Sir H. Herbert in his office-book on 3rd September, 1624, as a new play for the Cockpit Company " Written by Hayward."

The main plot is skilfully adapted from the *Rudens* (the *Rope*) of Plautus, the scene being shifted from Cyrene to Marseilles. The heroine, Palæstea, goes through perilous experiences in captivity to a brothel-keeper (like Marina in *Pericles*) and in shipwreck when she attempts to escape. But she is finally rescued, by an English merchant, Ashburne, who has come to Marseilles to find refuge from his creditors. A fisherman in his service catches with his rope a box which has been lost in the shipwreck. The fisherman claims this, anglicising the Plautine legal phrases, as " mine own, my lands, my goods, my copyhold, my fee—simple . . . Since fishing is free and the sea common." The box is found to contain a casket with property of Palæstea, proving that she is Ashburne's long lost daughter. He now bestows her hand on a faithful young lover, Raphael, while he himself receives the good news that he has inherited a fortune from an uncle.

But Heywood is never content with only one plot. He introduces a sub-plot, in which a Friar John pays court to the wife of the Duke of Averne and is strangled by the Duke and his man Dennis. They then prop up the body, as if alive, and when Friar Richard gives it a blow, it appears that he has murdered him. He carries the body to the door of the Duke who, helped by Dennis, puts it upon a stallion with a lance in its hand. The stallion chases a mare upon which Friar Richard has ridden forth, till in terror he announces that he has killed Friar John. Thereupon the Duke to save him confesses that he was the murderer and is pardoned by the King.

This story is taken with altered names from a *Novella* by Masuccio di Salerno. In the same year as *The Captives* was licensed by Herbert as a new play Heywood also told the story in prose in his Γυναικεῖον as concerning a lady in Norwich which he had often heard related as true.

The special interest attaching to this story both in its prose form and as a sub-plot in *The Captives* is its relation to a similar episode in Marlowe's *Jew of Malta*. Heywood himself in his epistle to Thomas Hammon prefixed to the only known edition of *The Jew* in 1633 stated that he " ushered it into the Court, and presented it to the Cock-pit, with these Prologues and Epilogues here inserted " :

The opening lines of both the Prologues are notable. That spoken at Court begins :

> Gracious and great, that we so boldly dare
> (Mongst other plays that now in fashion are)
> To present this, writ many years agone,
> And in that age thought seemd unto none,
> We humbly crave your pardon.

And that at the Cockpit :

> We know not how our play may pass this stage,
> But by the best of poets in that age,
> The *Malta-Jew* had being and was made,
> And he then by the best of actors play'd.

This was Edward Alleyn, the peerless, " Proteus for shapes, and Roscius for a tongue." Heywood evidently thinks that he is taking a risk in reviving an old-fashioned play, which largely owed its success to an incomparable actor, and it is likely that he did some editing. But did he insert, as F. G. Fleay and Dr. Clark have maintained, the whole of an episode which in some parts recalls the sub-plot of *The Captives*? The Jew in Act II ii, lures Friar Bernadine to his house and strangles him because he can prove his villainy. With the help of Ithamore the body is propped upon a staff and is thus encountered by Jacomo, a friar of a rival order, who strikes him down, and, believing that he has killed him, confesses his guilt and is executed. There are obvious parallels. But there are also important differences. There is no question in Marlowe's play of a love-intrigue. There is no mention of the stallion and the mare, and Jacomo instead of being pardoned is executed, and as Margarete Thimme has shown in her treatise on Marlowe's *Jew of Malta : Stil und Echtseitsfragen* (1921) there is no evidence of Heywood's characteristic vocabulary in this scene. Nor does Fräulein Thimme find such evidence in the scenes, also attributed to Heywood by Fleay, in which the Courtesan Bellamira is the chief figure.*

It was not to Roman comedy but to Roman legendary history, as related by Livy, that Heywood was chiefly indebted in *The Rape of Lucrece* published first in 1608, as acted by the Queen's servants at the Red Bull. Heywood had also with little doubt also a debt to Shakespeare whose *Lucrece* had been reprinted in 1607, and

---

*To those who wish to pursue the matter further I would recommend Appendix III of Clark's *Thomas Heywood*, and the appendix to the chapter on *The Jew of Malta* in my own *Christopher Marlowe* (1940).

whose *Macbeth* dating about 1606, seems to have suggested the opening scene where Tarquin's wife, Tullia, prompts his criminal ambition after a cruder fashion than Lady Macbeth's with her husband's.

Tar.	What would'st thou, wife.
Tull.	Be what I am not, make thee greater far
	Than thou can'st aim to be . . . O me, I am
	sick !
Tar.	Sick, lady ?
Tull.	Sick at heart.
Tar.	Why, my sweet Tullia ?
Tull.	To be a queen, I long, long, and am sick.
Tar.	Hear me, wife.
Tull.	I am no wife of Tarquin, if not king.
	Oh had Jove made me man, I would have
	mounted
	Above the base tribunals of the earth
	Up to the clouds, for pompous sovereignty.
	Thou art a man ; oh bear my royal mind,
	Mount heaven, and see if Tullia lag behind.

She should more truly have said " Descend to Hell," for the way to the throne lies through the murder of her aged father Servius which is accomplished in the Capitol, where his dead body is trodden underfoot by her. How different here from Lady Macbeth who would herself have murdered Duncan had he not resembled her father as he slept. Tarquin enthroned assumes totalitarian power more absolute than that claimed by the Stuart kings.

> We challenge too, by our prerogative,
> The goods of such as strive against our state.
> The freest citizens, without attaint,
> Arraign or judgment we to **exile** doom.

Tullia echoes this with an unequivocal assertion of royal divine right. " Kings are as gods and divine sceptres bear."

By the advice of Collatinus, husband of Lucrece, the Roman nobles, to deceive Tarquin, indulge in harmless sports, " hawk, hunt game, sing, dance," and stay the time till the hour for revenge is ripe. It is Collatinus too who, when at a merry-meeting in the camp before Arden the merits of wives are being debated, proposes :

> Let's mount our steeds,
> And to our houses all come unprepared,
> And unexpected by our high-praised wives.
> She of them all that we find best employed,
> Devoted and most housewife-exercised,
> Let her be held most virtuous, and her husband
> Win by the wager a rich horse and armour.

They find Lucrece at night " teaching her servants sundry ' chores '," and by the verdict of Tarquin's son Sextus she wins the prize for her husband. But by the irony of fate Collatinus' successful wager—and it is a dramatic link that should not be overlooked—leads to his wife's undoing. Sextus inflamed by her beauty returns by night to her house and in a scene where Lucrece, in contrast with the wives of Shore, Frankford, and Wincott, faces death rather than dishonour, achieves his vile purpose. In her agonised cry :

> Is it my fate above all other women,
> Or is my sin more heinous than the rest,
> That among thousands, millions, infinites,
> I, only I, should to this shame be born,
> To be a stain to women, nature's scorn ?—

Heywood again shows his mastery of poignant utterance. She lives only to tell the tale of her wrongs, and to hear the Roman leaders swear to avenge her, and then takes her own life. The sequel is too long drawn-out, with Horatius of the Tiber bridge, Scævola of the burnt hand, and the Etruscan Porsenna pushed chronologically ahead, to bring in those spectacular fighting episodes so dear to Elizabethan theatre-goers.

Unfortunately however Heywood made a more reprehensible concession to the taste of the audience at the Red Bull which catered largely for what we would now call " low-brows." A merry Roman lord, Valerius, is made to spend his time in singing an extraordinary medley of songs quite irrelevant to the Tarquin-Lucrece plot. This includes one or two fine songs, " Now what is love I will thee tell " and " Pack clouds away and welcome day." But most of them are very frolicsome ditties, like the one beginning " Shall I woo the lovely Molly," another concerning the taverns of Rome, really those of London, and another describing the costumes and drinks of the various nations. Thus on to a tragic historical play was incongruously grafted an element of comic opera, including what shocks us now, a ribald catch for three voices on the rape itself. Yet all this was evidently popular. The 1608 quarto of the play was followed by two in 1609 and others in 1630 and 1638. The last contained an epilogue with a couple of new songs " added by the stranger that lately acted Valerius his part." One of these gives the cries of Rome, really those of London, of which the following verse is the most glaring example.

> Bread-and-meat—bread-and-meat, for the tender mercy of God to the poor prisoners of Newgate, four-score-and-ten poor prisoners.
> Thus, go the cries in Rome's fair town,
> First they go up street, and then they go down.

Another play on a subject from the early legendary history of Rome, *Appius and Virginia*, was printed in 1654, for Richard Marriot who ascribed it on the title-page to John Webster. But these posthumous attributions of plays by publishers in the seventeenth century are often not to be trusted. There is now a general consensus among critics that Heywood had more than a finger in the tragedy while Rupert Brooke went so far as to claim it for him entirely.

The problem of authorship is complicated by that of date, on which widely differing views have been put forward. If this play is mainly from Heywood's pen it would be reasonable to assume that it followed soon after *The Rape of Lucrece* about 1610 and it seems not to have been sufficiently noted that in the closing speech of *Appius and Virginia* the heroines of the two tragedies are linked together, as would be specially be-fitting by a dramatist who had presented them both on the stage.

> Two Ladies fair, but most unfortunate,
> Have in their ruins rais'd declining Rome—
> Lucretia and Virginia, both renown'd
> For Chastity

Virtuous womanhood in both cases ready to suffer death rather than dishonour from a tyrant's lust makes a special appeal to Heywood, and the handling of the action is in his forthright fashion without the subtler overtones characteristic of Webster. Prominent in both plays are the camp scenes, which are the invention of the dramatist. And in the singularly dispassionate attitude of Virginius to Appius in Act V it may not be fanciful to see something of a parallel to Frankford's towards his wife in *A Woman Killed with Kindness*. If the pleading of the Orator in the trial scene (IV. 1) is reminiscent of Webster, the speech of Virginius before he kills his daughter has the pathos and tenderness of Heywood.

> Let me forget the thought
> Of thy most pretty infancy, when first
> Returning from the wars, I took delight
> To rock thee in my target, when my girl
> Would kiss her father in his burgonet*
> Of glittering steel hung 'bout his armed neck,
> And viewing the bright metal, smile to see
> Another fair Virginia smile on thee.

But even if the more imponderable evidences of style may be deceptive, the conclusive argument in my opinion for Heywood's hand in the play is the solid one of vocabulary. He has a fondness for coining and repeating out-of-the-way words. Among those occurring in *Appius and Virginia* and other of his writings are " infallid "=infallible, " palped "=palpable, " imposterous "=imposturing, " comragne "=comrade, " torved "=fierce. These could easily be multiplied† but they are sufficient to prove Heywood's case as at any rate part author of the play.

*Helmet.

†See F. L. Lucas's Introduction to and commentary on *Appius and Virginia*, Vol. III of his edition of Webster, and A. M. Clark, *op. cit.*, Appendix I.

CHAPTER 5

Troia Britannica or Great Britain's Troy

In 1609 Heywood produced his first important
original work, not in dramatic form, *Troia Britannica
or Great Britain's Troy* was described on the title-page as
" A Poem divided into XVII several Cantos inter-
mixed with many pleasant Poetical Tales. Concluding
with an universal Chronicle from the Creation until
these present times." Heywood may thus be said, in a
variant of Bacon's dictum, to have taken all historical
knowledge for his province. The poem was a folio of
466 pages, mainly in *ottava rima*, and was printed by
William Jaggard. Heywood later in an epistle to
Archibald Okes appended to *An Apology for Actors* complained bitterly of the " infinite faults " that had
escaped notice in the printing. But anyone acquainted
with Heywood's baffling script will make allowance
for Jaggard.

The poem has an extremely modest verse dedication
to the Earl of Worcester,

> Whose favour gave my Muse first breath
> To try in th'air her weak unable wing.

But in stanzas 8 and 9 of Canto I there is what is virtu-
ally a second dedication to King James and his Court.

> O may these artless numbers in your ears,
> (Renowned James) seem musically strung.
> Your fame (oh, Jove's-starr'd Prince) spread every-
> where,

First gave my still and speechless Muse a tongue,
From your majestic virtues, prised dear,
The infant life of these harsh metres sprung.
  Oh, take not then their industry in scorn,
  Who, but to emblaze you, had been yet unborn.

Nor let your princely Peers hold in disdain
To have their ancestry styl'd and enrolled
In this poor register ; a higher strain
Their merits ask, since brazen leaves unfold
Their never-dying fame, yet thus much deign
Not to despise to hear your virtues told
  In a plain style by one whose wish and heart
  Supplies in zeal want both of skill and art.

The first seven Cantos, beginning with the Creation
and with " the golden world, the purest age," follow
the course of classical mythology to the labours of
Hercules. In the eighth Troy in its flourishing state
under Priam is described, and in nine and the earlier
part of ten Heywood forsakes for a time his *ottava rima*
to insert love-letters interchanged between Paris and
Helen translated from Ovid's *Heroides* in five-foot
couplets, as Turberville had done in different metre
forty-two years before.

Then follows to Canto XV the account of the
siege and fall of Troy, with the return of the victorious
Agamemnon and his murder. Here Heywood relies
not upon Homer but on Roman and medieval sources
which (as the title of the poem indicates) link Britain
with Troy. Thus in Canto XVI the landing of Brute,
the grandson of Aeneas, on its shores is described in
detail, with a marginal note of the date as 2855 from
the Creation and 1108 B.C. (st. 9).

Prince Brute with Corineus doth Albion enter,
At Totnes, thirty monstrous giants kills,

And after much and dangerous adventer
Builds London (called New Troy) ; his throne he fills
Twenty four yeares, then pays his last debenter
To Nature, Britain he to Locrine wills,
    Scotland to Albanact ; Wales Camber sways ;
    Israel was judg'd by Samuel in their days.

In the last line, in almost casual fashion, Biblical and
British history are brought parallel, and in stanza
35 they are set side by side, together with Roman,
in still more surprising fashion.

Hortensius, Livy, Sallust, Ovid all
Were fam'd in Rome : valiant Guiderius next
The Britons as their sovereign Liege install.
Twenty-eight years he governs, much perplext
With Roman wars ; now chanced Sejanus fall
Under Tiberius ; now, as saith the text,
John Baptist preached, and by King Herod died :
Pilate was Judge, and Christ was crusified.

That the central and most solemn event in world history should thus be disposed of in half a line takes our
breath away, though there was no thought of
irreverence on Heywood's part. When he comes down
to Elizabeth nothing could be more pious than his
farewell to his departed sovereign.

I leave her shrin'd 'mongst angels, there to sing
Unending praises to th'eternal King.

The ninety-five stanzas of the Canto trace the
legendary and semi-historical record of the British
monarchy to the victory of William of Normandy over
Harold at Hastings. The final Canto XVII is " a
brief index or short register " of events in England and

abroad from the Norman Conquest to the accession of James I.

In so protracted a poem covering in Heywood's discursive fashion largely derivative material of such varied type there are inevitably inequalities and *longeurs*. It needed the genius of a Byron in a later age to acclimatise fully the *ottava rima* in English prosody. But there are many narrative and descriptive passages in which Heywood shows remarkable pictorial gifts and a mastery over rhythmical and verbal effects. Some instances may here be given. In the account of the rape of Proserpine by Pluto there is a dazzling contrast between the flower-laden damsel and the dark God of the underworld with his black chariot and steeds (VI, 105-6)

Hither fair Proserpine repairing still
With daisies, daffodils and lilies white,
Roses and marigolds, her lap to fill,
And to return home laden (a sweet sight),
Chaplets to make, or garlands by fine skill,
By chance the God of shades in edge of night
    In his black ebon chariot hurrying by
    Upon the virgin casts a ravisher's eye.

*   *   *   *   *

He spies, and loves, and catches up at ones*
Th' affrighted virgin, who lets fall her flowers ;
He bears her over hills, dales, rocks and stones
She calls on mother, friends and tears she powers ;†
Mother nor friend can hear her shrieks and groans,
Through pools and lakes the God of Tartar scours,‡
    He yerks§ his hot steeds with his wiry strings,
    And from his coach-wheels misty darkness flings

*   *   *   *   *

*Once. †Pours. ‡Hastens. §Flogs.

And calls his jetty stallions by their names,
Whose hard hoofs make the vaulted centre sound ;
His rattling chariot through the air proclaims
His fear and flight, with burnished brass shod round.
Not once looks back the dreadful God of flames,
Or thinks his rape safe on the upper ground,
But with his ebon mace the earth enforces,
Which cleft sinks him, his chariot and his horses.

The effective use of detail, emphasised by resonant
monosyllabic words, reappears in the description of
the tempest which almost wrecks the Argonauts in their
voyage, and which suggests that Heywood is speaking
from personal experience (VII, 44 ff.).

At the black evening close the sea looked white,
The storm-presaging wave begins to swell,
And blustering Eurus rising now at night
With his flag wings upon the waters fell,
The Master bids slack sail, but 'gainst the might
Of his commanded mates the winds rebel :
The boatswain brawls,* the mariners are chid,
For what they would the stubborn gusts forbid.

*   *   *   *   *

All fall to labour, one man helps to steer,
Others to slacken the big-bellied sail.
Some to the capstring† call, some pray, some swear,
Some let the tackles slip, while others hale :
Some cling unto the main mast and cleave there,
Some chafe with anger, some with fear look pale :
Some ply the pump and (that which would devour
Their ship in time) sea into sea repour.

*   *   *   *   *

Now, as the sinking billows are divided,
Low valleys 'tween too mighty mountains fall,

*Scolds.   †Capstan.

From whose steep breasts the shaken vessel slided,
Burying at sea sails, tackles, masts and all,
But there remains not long ; the bark well guided
Climbs up those cliffs, a dreadful watery wall,
 That to themselves amaz'd with fear they show
 Like men in th'air surveying Hell below.

There is something of Heywood's dramatic quality in
Medea's distracted self-communing before she decides
to enable Jason to win the golden fleece and to become
his bride in a far-off land. (VII, 65-6.)

But how, Medea, wilt thou then forsake
Thy country, father, friends, all which are great,
And to thy lord a roving pirate take
One that perchance hath no abiding seat ?
Fond* girl ! thou wrong'st him these faint doubts
 to make,
A royal prince and in all acts complete.
 Thy country, father, friends, trifles but small,
 And this one warlike Jason worth them all.

  * * * * *

That he is lovely witnesseth mine eye,
And valiant, what can better record bear
Than this attempt, whose fame to heaven will fly,
T'amaze the Gods that shall this novel† hear ?
I leave a barren Kingdom, to descry
A populous nation, what then should I fear ?
 In seeking with this amorous Greek to dwell
 I ask Elisium in exchange for Hell.

Heywood's fondness for detail, especially physical,
shows to less advantage in his attempts at portraiture,
as, for instance, in part of his description of Hector
(VIII, 28-9).

     *Foolish. †News.

Hector, the eldest of King Priam's race,
Past in his puissance all Knights of that age,
An able body, and a pleasant face,
Affable, and not much inclined to rage,
Big-limb'd, but featur'd well, which added grace
To his proportion, young, but gravely sage :
 His flesh tough-hard but white, his blue veins airy,
 His quick eye fiery bright ; his skin much hairy,
  * * * * *
His head short-curl'd, his beard an auburn brown,
His pleasant language lisping, but not loud ;
Save in the wars he was not seen to frown ;
Save to his God and King he never bow'd :
In field a lion, but a lamb in town,
Strong without equal, but in arms not proud,
 Was never known to speak felonious word,
 Or but against Troy's foes to use a sword.

And who would recognise the Helen of Doctor Faustus's enraptured vision in this Helen " of the golden mean," with its prosaic equation of opposite extremes ? Well may Heywood apologise for his " ragged quill." (X, 31-2.)

She was nor dwarf-like statur'd nor too tall,
Nor foggy* fat, nor yet consumptive lean ;
Her waist not gross, nor yet too slender-small,
Her fair proportion was smooth, quaint and clean :
Her habit shadowed no extreme at all,
She was all shaped by the golden mean,
 So rare that never eye dwelt on her cheek
 But lost itself and had his light to seek.

What should I with harsh language slubber o'er
Exact perfection ? Shall my ragged quill
In seeking Nature's cunning to explore
Injure the work in which she shows such skill ?
     *Flabby.

Loues Schoole.

PVBLII
OVIDII NASONIS
DE ARTE AMANDI.
Or
The Art of
Loue.

Gedruckt tot Amsterdam by Nicolas Iansz. Visscher

Title page of the English translation of Ovid's *Ars Amatoria*.

TROIA BRITANICA:

OR,

Great Britaines Troy.

A Poem

Deuided into XVII. seuerall Cantons, intermixed
with many pleasant Poeticall Tales.

Concluding with an Vniuersall Chronicle from the Creation,
vntill these present Times.

Written ly Tho: Heywood.

Et prodesse solent, & Delectare Poeta.

LONDON,
Printed by W. Jaggard, 1609.

Title page of *Troia Britannica* or *Great Britain's Troy.*

T'express such graces as the Gods adore
In Helen would a spacious volume fill,
  And ask (should I her beauties all recite)
  A world of paper and an age to write.

But if Heywood faltered in the attempt to depict **Helen**,
and if even, as has been seen, he had recourse to translation in expressing the passion between her and **Paris**,
he could in curiously indirect fashion interpret the
overpowering tyranny of love. In Canto V he puts
into the mouth of Jupiter (sts. 66–76) a reply to those
who censored the God for the number of his amours.
Here is part of his *apologia*.

I love, but yet I know not in what fashion ;
I love a thousand, for a thousand reasons,
My moving thoughts abide in no firm station ;
My heart is subject to my blind thoughts' treasons.
For every sundry lass I enter passion,
And am of love provided at all seasons :
  That wench is modest ? oh, she's in my books,
  I only love her for her modest looks.

　　*　　　*　　　*　　　*　　　*

Is she a scholar ? then her art delights me :
Is she a dunce ? her simpleness contents me :
Doth she applaud my love ? her praise incites me,
Or discommend me ? yet she represents me
With matter of new love. Admit she spites me,
I love her, for her spite no whit torments me,
  For though her words be rough, smooth is her skin,
  What in the first I love, the last, I win.

　　*　　　*　　　*　　　*　　　*

Is her hair brown ? so lovely Leda's was,
Brown tramelled locks best grace the brightest hue.
Are her locks yellow ? such Aurora's glass
Presents in her attiring to her view ?

Is [her] hair orient bright. It doth surpass ;
If chestnut-coloured, such do I pursue :
    My eyes still aim at beauties' rare perfections,
    And I all colours love, and all complexions.

Though Jupiter speaks these lines, they would be
equally fitting from the lips of any rake of the Jacobean
age. They may therefore serve as a bridge to some of
the numerous topical passages with which Heywood
catches the perhaps straying attention of his readers.
Thus he begins Canto III with a panegyric on the
benefits conferred on England by King James in his
rôle as a peace-maker.

When I record the dire effects of war,
I cannot but with happy praise admire
The blessed friends of peace which smooths the fear
Of wounding steel and all-consuming fire.
Oh, in what safety then thy subjects are,
Royal King James, secur'd from war's fierce ire,
    That by thy peaceful government alone
    Studiest divided Christendom t'atone.

        *   *   *   *   *

Thy liegemen thou has plac'd as on a hill
Free from the cannon's reach from far to see
Divided nations one another kill,
Whilst thy safe people as spectators be,
Only to take a view what blood they spill,
They near to ruin, yet in safety we
    Alone in peace, whilst all the realms about us
    Envy our bliss, yet forced to fight without us.

Heywood adds a somewhat curious comparison of the
Kentish men who viewed the defeat of the Armada from
the shore, but unwillingly could not take a part in it.

So stood the Kentish men to view the main
In the year eighty-eight when th' English fleet
Fought with the huge Armadas brought from Spain,
With what impatience did they stand to see't
On the safe shore, willing to leave the train
Of such faint cowards as think safety sweet
    In such a quarrel where invaders threat us,
    And in our native Kingdom seek to beat us.

And Heywood is thus led on to pay tributes to Howard,
England's Admiral, Hawkins, Frobisher and Drake,
" Whose very name made Spain's armadas quake."
    An earlier English triumph over another more power-
ful foe is recalled by the use for the first time by the
followers of Saturn of bows and arrows in their battle
with the giants (II, 59).

Thou famous English Henry of that name
The fifth : I cannot but remember thee
That won unto thy Kingdom endless fame
By thy bold English archers' chivalry
In Agincourt, when to the Frenchmen's shame
King, Dauphin, and the chief Nobility
    Were with the odds of thousands forced to yield,
    And Henry lord of that triumphant field.

Then Heywood when describing the sea fight between
Jove with his Centaurs and the pirates of the Aegean
Sea acclaims Sir Richard Grenville (V, 44-5).

        To this I may compare
Thy boarding, valiant Greenvild, thou didst brook
A hotter skirmish than the Pirates dare,
Who keeping one good ship scorn'st to be took
By a whole fleet of Spanish man-a-war,
    Fighting till powder, shot and men were wasted,
    And these consum'd, even till thine own life lasted.

As often as they boarded thee, so oft,
Bravely repulsed, their sides bored through and
  through,
And three times with thy three decks blown aloft,
As high as heaven (what more could valour do ?)
Now thy proud ship hath all her ensigns doft,
Those sails the amorous winds with courtings woo
  To tinder burnt : thou proferr'd life despising
  Leav'st thy *Revenge* even with the waters rising.

And as Heywood, in the opening scene of *The Fair Maid
of the West, Part I,* pictured Essex and his company
setting forth in 1597 on their island voyage to the
Azores he now compares his enterprise to that of Jason
with the Argonauts in quest of the golden fleece.
(VII, 51.)

As brave a general marshalled our great fleet,
As that bold Greek that sought the fleece of gold,
Hoping by sea an enemy to meet
Fiercer than Jason's, and more warlike bold,
Renowned Essex, at whose warlike feet
Spain's countless spoils and trophies have been told,
  Who from Hesperia brought to England's Greece
  More gold than would have weigh'd down Jason's
  fleece.

And later in the same Canto (st. 87) he compares the
taking of Cadiz first by Drake and then by Essex to the
capture of Troy by Hercules.
  But Heywood is evidently divided between his desire to celebrate the heroic actions of his countrymen
and to pay tribute to the pacific policy of James which
he had already hymned at the opening of Canto III,
and which he compares to the league to end war between Jupiter and Troos, first King of Troy (VI, 49).

'Twixt England and great Spain, two potent nations,
Like enmity hath long time been commenced,
And whilst Eliza liv'd her proclamations
Oppos'd their pride and her own province fenced.
But now with mutual kind congratulations
All injuries on both sides are dispensed ;
 And our great England's Jove for Spain's best use
 Hath at their suit granted a termine* truce.

In a somewhat irrelevant but forcible interlude in his
narrative (IV, 42–9) Heywood expatiates on the all-
powerful influence of Opinion, especially in the political
and religious spheres. Thence he is led on to a detailed
picture of it in one contemporary form. (IV, 50–4.)

In our reformed church too a new man
Is in few years crept up, in strange disguise,
And called the self-opinion'd Puritan ;
A fellow that can bear himself precise :
No church supremacy endure he can,
No orders in the Bishop's diocese :
 He keeps a starched gait, wears a formal ruff,
 A nosegay, set face, and a poted† cuff.

He never bids " God speed you," on the way
Because he knows not what your bosoms smother,
His phrase is " Verily : By yea and nay,"
" In faith, in truth, good neighbour, or good
 brother,"
And when he borrows money, ne'er will pay,
One of th'elect must common with another,
 And when the poor his charity entreat :
 " You labour not, and therefore must not eat."

He will not preach but lecture, nor in white,
Because the Elders of the Church command it.
He will no cross in baptism ; none shall fight

*A truce settling disputes. †Crimped.

Under that banner, if he may withstand it ;
Nor out of ancient Fathers Latin cite ;
The cause may be he doth not understand it.
    His followers preach all faith and by their works
    You would not judge them Catholics but Turks.

He can endure no organs but is vext
To hear the quiristers shrill anthems sing :
He blames degrees in th'Academy next,
And 'gainst the liberal arts can Scripture bring ;
And when his tongue hath run beside the best,
You may perceive him his loud clamours ring
    'Gainst honest pastimes, and with piteous phrase
    Rail against hunting, hawking, cocks and plays.

With these the Brownists in some points cohere,
That likewise hold the marriage ring profane ;
Commanded prayers they'll not endure to hear,
And to subscribe to canons they disdain.
They hold more sin a corner'd cap to wear.
Than cut a purse. Leave these as wild and vain.
    By thee Opinion, realms have been confounded
    What dar'st not thou, when thou art firmly
        grounded ?

The last couplet might almost seem to be a prophetic
forecast of the Civil War, waged on both sides for
" Opinion," in Heywood's wide interpretation of the
word. And had not these caustic stanzas been embedded
in an unfamiliar poem far apart from seventeenth
century sectarian controversy they would have become,
as they deserve to be, a classic presentation of the
Puritans and their fellow travellers.

As if to emphasise the distance between himself and
these haters of the arts Heywood begins Canto VII
with an impassioned tribute to Music.

Music, by which the spheres are taught to move,
And tune their motion to their Maker's praise,
Approves itself divine : first found above,
After bequeath'd frail man, to cheer his days :
Whether t'were taught as by the birds, that prove
Their harmony in their sweet-chirping lays,
 Or whether found by man ; of this I am sure
 It hath been ancient, and shall long endure.

Then after a highly doubtful chronicle of the invention
of the chief instruments Heywood stresses the paradox
of music's conflicting powers.

This, as it hath the power in dreadful wars
'Mongst soft effeminate breasts to kindly rage,
And to relenting grace all entrance bars,
So hath it power the rudest thoughts t'assuage.
To music move the planets, dance the stars,
It tempers fury, makes the wild man sage.
 In this consent of strings he that can well
 May with harmonious Orpheus enter hell.

Similarly but at greater length in the fifteen opening
stanzas of Canto VIII he hymns the marvellous influence of " Fair Poesic, both ancient and divine."
After a roll-call of sacred and classical poets he celebrates poetry as the great preserver and creator.

A poem is the richest monument,
And only lives when marble tombe decay,
Showing Kings' deeds, their merit and descent,
Not stabb'd by time, whom sepulchres obey,
Thou proud Achilles with thy great ostent,
Where stands thy monumental grave this day ?
 Tomb-makers die disgraced, then Homer trust,
 By whom thy fame lives, now thy grave is dust.

  * * * * *

Poets are makers ; had great Homer pleased,
Penelope had been wanton, Helen chaste,
The Spartan King the mutinous host appeased,
And smooth Ulysses with the horn disgrac'd.
Thersites had the imperial sceptre seized,
And Agamemnon in his rank been plac'd,
   O Homer ! 'twas in thee Troy to subdue,
   Thy pen, not Greece, the Trojans overthrew.

Heywood therefore warns evil-doers to enlist poets
on their side (VIII, 11).

Art thou a tyrant ? to thy service take
Some Helieonian scholar, whose fine quill
To after times thy reign may gentle make,
And give them life, whom thou in rage didst kill.
Art thou a usurer ? Wilt thou not forsake
A hundred for a hundred ? Learn this skill,
   To some one fluent poet pension give,
   And he shall make thy famous bounty live.

    *   *   *   *   *

Art thou a coward ? Exhibitions lend
To scholars that shall make the Muse thy friend,
Art thou a glutton ? make thee ventrous bold* ;
Or a loose lecher ? give thy poet gold,
He'll clear thy fame, and give thy scandal end,
He can redeem renown to ruin sold,
   Make rioters forget, the dull blind to see,
   The drunkard temperate, and the covetous free.

And following his own precept he begins Canto XI
with a celebration of the great deeds of British cham-
pions, " above the Greeks in the high tower of fame,"
from the legendary Brennus and Nennius down to the
Elizabethans, " Howard, Grey, Norris, Sidney, Essex,
Vere." And in a couplet incidentally betraying the

               *Valiant with the belly.

traditional superior valuation of the Trojans as compared with their foes Heywood adds :

> These, had they liv'd in aged Priam's days,
> Had dimmed the Greeks' and matched the Trojans'
> praise.

Thence he passes in stanzas 9 to 17 to describe the
Palace of Fame* set in the world's navel. In illustration
of his mastery of detail even in such a fanciful picture
stanzas 13 and 14 may be quoted :

> Infinite cursors,† pursevants,‡ aid posts,
> Ambassadors, and such as hurry news,
> Heralds (such men as traffic between hosts),
> Walk to and fro, and no man tales eschews,
> One speaks of wars, of combats, and rude boasts,
> Another serious talk of peace pursues :
> > All as they are dispos'd ; this man is telling
> > Of buying land, that other speaks of selling.
>
> > *   *   *   *   *
>
> Some talk of this man's honours, that man's shames,
> Others of storms, and many a boisterous flaw, §
> Some men of their success and chance in games,
> One what he heard, another what he saw ;
> Some men of knights adventurers, some of dames,
> Others how long their suits have hung in law.
> > Toys with things serious pass, grave things with
> > bables ‖,
> > Lies mixed with truths, and truths discoursed with
> > fables.

Heywood himself would not have been out of place in
this palace of fame. Having talked of the honours of
British worthies he turns in Canto XV to denounce

---

*In the sense of the Latin *Fama* or Renown.
†Couriers.   ‡Pursuivants.   §Squall.   ‖Baubles.

the shames of British traitors, Parry, Babington, and
" Gui Vaux " (Guy Fox), compared with whom the
Greek Sinon was a saint.

> He told a forg'd tale to a foreign King,
> With hope his King and country's fame to raise,
> But thou from strangers didst thy complots bring ;
> He a strange country, not his own betrays.

Heywood would have done better to rest content with
branding the infamy of Guy Faux, without adding a
prayer destined to be so bitterly mocked during his own
lifetime (st. 8).

> That the same state that was in hazard then
> May in this peaceful Kingdom long endure ;
> The King to guide his Peers ; Peers, Common men,
> Whose summon'd Parliaments may plant secure
> Britain's fair [peace,]* for many a worthy pen
> To chronicle.

Whether or not Heywood had any real doubt that his
own was a worthy pen, he closed his long poetic survey
with a modest apology.

> If I have any way failed the reader's expectation
> by inserting things frivolous, or omitting things
> material, I must excuse it thus that I have more will
> than art and more endeavour than cunning . . . only
> this much let me speak in mine own behalf ; with
> ages past I have been too little acquainted, and with
> this age present I dare not be too bold.

But whatever its merits or otherwise, *Troia Britannica*
was his own and he was not ready to see any part of it
sailing under false colours. In the same epistle to Okes
in which he complained of the faulty printing of *Troia*

---

*" Peere " in the text : ? misprint for " peace."

Britannica, he also resented " the manifest injury done me in that work by taking the Epistles of Paris to Helen and Helen to Paris and printing them in a less volume under the name of another, which may put the world in opinion I might steal from him, and he to do himself right hath since published them in his own name." The " less volume " was the third edition of *The Passionate Pilgrim* (1612), an anthology published by William Jaggard under Shakespeare's name, with the two Epistles (Cantos IX and X of *Troia Britannica*) and other Heywood pieces added. Heywood further states that he knows that " the author " was " much offended with Mr. Jaggard that altogether unknown to him presumed to make so bold with his name." The protest was not without effect for in the later printing of this edition of *The Passionate Pilgrim* Shakespeare's name was omitted.

CHAPTER 6

Translations of Sallust—An Apology for Actors

In 1608 Heywood's classical interest found expression in a new way, prose translation. He published an English version of " the two most worthy and notable histories " of Sallust, *The Conspiracy of Catiline* and *The War of Jugurtha*. Like other Elizabethan translators he was dependent, at any rate in part, on an intermediary between himself and the original. Charles Whibley in his introduction to the reprint of Heywood's version in " The Tudor Translations " (1524) proved that in various instances he was following not the Latin of Sallust but the French rendering by Loys Meignet Lyonnois. And the long preparatory epistle to the courteous reader, " Of the Choice of History," occupying forty-three pages of the reprint, is lifted from the fourth chapter of Jean Bodin's *Methodus ad facilem historiarum eognitionem*, with nothing more than Bodin's name in the margin, and, in connection with a mention of Froissart, a footnote to the effect that " the author himself was a Frenchman."

In his dedication to Sir Thomas Somerset, a son of the Earl of Worcester, Heywood states that he undertook the work " for the pleasure of your vacant hours but especially for the general good of all English gentlemen." It is comprehensible that in a period of conspiracies, when that of Gowrie and the Gunpowder Plot were recent, the story of Catiline, soon to be dramatised by Ben Jonson, could have had some lessons

[76]

for English gentlemen, but the war with Jugurtha can scarcely have touched them nearly.

In any case Heywood judged by the standard of his time, proved himself a capable translator. He reproduces faithfully enough in the main the meaning of Sallust, and when he explains some of the phrases in the original, or gives them a very vernacular rendering, he adds to the interest of his version for latter day readers. At the same time the interpretation, even at second hand, of Sallust's mannered style was a useful discipline for Heywood's too facile pen.

Heywood's next published excursion into prose was far apart from the translation of Sallust, though it bears many marks of classical lore. Probably first taken in hand about 1608, *An Apology for Actors* was printed by Nicholas Okes in 1612. *Apology* has here not its modern but its original Greek meaning, Heywood was not presenting an excuse for the men of his profession but a defence of them. The *Apology* represents a phase in the long conflict between the opponents, chiefly but not entirely, Puritans, of the theatre and its supporters. The earlier history of that conflict, in which Gosson, Lodge, Gager, and Reynolds are prominent figures, has been summarised by Dr. Dover Wilson in a chapter in Volume VI of *The Cambridge History of English Literature*.

Why exactly at this particular time, and against whom in particular Heywood took up the cudgels on behalf of his " quality "—the technical term of the period for the acting profession—is not known, nor does his dedicatory epistle to the Earl of Worcester throw light on this.

In his prefatory address to his " good Friends and Fellows, the City actors "—he speaks of sparing some time for this particular purpose " out of my busiest hours," and in a further address to the judicial reader he declares that he would not have ventured on it " but that a kind of necessity enjoined me to so sudden a business." As far as is known there had been something of a pause in the controversy at this time.

How far Heywood's protest that he is the youngest and weakest of the nest wherein he was hatched, and that he thought it better " to stammer out my mind than not to speak at all " is merely mock-modesty is difficult to say. By 1612 he must have had about sixteen years' experience as actor and playwright, and few, except Shakespeare himself, whom Heywood never mentions in his pamphlet, could have been better qualified for the task. And it is indeed the parts of it, often in illustration of some general statement, which are the fruit of his own experience that give the *Apology* its chief value today.

He divides it into three brief treatises (1) The antiquity of actors, (2) their ancient dignity, (3) the true use of their quality. But the three parts run to some extent with one another and are buttressed with a plentiful display of classical references and precedents. In his main argument, which combines the defence of actors and the stage generally, Heywood, like previous apologists, rests his case upon the direct moral influence of the theatre, against which the Puritans could put up a strong counter-case. This was a customary weakness in Renaissance criticism of the drama, which did not emphasise its elevating appeal to the imaginations and to the aesthetic sense.

There is a *reductio ad absurdum* of this moral plea in the first of the instances cited by Heywood. Hercules in his nonage " had presented unto him by his tutor, in the fashion of a history acted by the choice of the nobility of Greece, the worthy and memorable acts of his father Jupiter ; which being presented with lively and well spirited action, wrought such impression on his noble thoughts . . . he perform'd his twelve labours.''

Then after stressing the influence of heroic stage spectacles on Alexander and Caesar he turns to '' our domestic histories,'' and the effect produced on any of English blood by seeing the person of any bold Englishman presented on the stage.

Then Heywood strikes a more original and interesting note. In the time of Christ there were '' spacious theatres in the greatest opinion among the Romans ; yet neither Christ himself, nor any of his sanctified apostles, in any of their sermons, acts, or documents, so much as named them, or upon any abusive occasion touched them.'' Why then, he asks,

> Should any nice* and over-scrupulous heads, since they cannot ground their curiossness† either upon the old or New Testament, take upon them to correct, control,‡ or carp at that, against which they cannot find any text in the sacred Scriptures.

This was indeed an effective way of turning their own weapons against the Puritan enemies of the theatre.

In his second treatise on the ancient dignity of actors Heywood cites copiously from the classical histories. But what interests us now are his allusions not to the ancient players but to those of his own period—to the English companies in the pay of Frederick II of Denmark (Queen Anne's father) '' commended unto him by the honourable the Earl of Leicester '' and of two German potentates. He speaks appreciatively of six

* Dainty.   †Fastidiousness.   ‡Contradict.

actors by name, who were before his time. To them he adds Tarleton, favourite both with his sovereign and the people, who has been succeeded in both respects by Will Kempe. He also pays tributes to contemporaries recently dead, Gabriel Spencer, Singer, Pope, Phillips and Sly, " whose deserts live in the remembrance of many," and to one yet alive, " in his time the most worthy, famous Master Edward Alleyn." We would gladly have had further details about all of these and spared for them allusions to the classical stage. Yet one of these leads up to what is for me as an editor of Kyd the most valuable reference in the whole *Apology*. Heywood recalls that Julius Caesar and later Roman emperors enjoyed acting themselves, and adds : Therefore, G. M. Kyd in his *Spanish Tragedy*, upon occasion presenting itself, thus writes :

> Why, Nero thought it no disparagement,
> And Kings and emperors have ta'en delight
> To make experience of their wits in plays.

The Spanish Tragedy ranks with *Tamburlaine* as the two most epoch-making of pre-Shakespearian plays, yet both appeared anonymously in all their editions, and it is solely from this reference by Heywood that we know that Thomas Kyd was the author of *The Spanish Tragedy*.

There are other plays and performances, with edifying consequences, to which Heywood alludes. The Earl of Sussex's men at King's Lynn in Norfolk acted *The History of Friar Francis* in which a woman who had murdered her husband was haunted by his ghost. Whereupon a woman of good reputation in the audience cried out " O my husband my husband ! I see the ghost of my husband fiercely thrusting and menacing me," and afterwards confessed that she had poisoned her husband seven years ago. A similar incident at a performance by English actors in Amsterdam of *The Four Sons of Aymon* leading to a woman's confession of the murder of her husband is also related. And strangest of all, during the performance of a battle on the stage at Perin in Cornwall the noise of the drums and trumpets frightened away a company of invading Spanish soldiers. Sir E. K. Chambers thinks that this was probably the abortive Spanish attempt to burn Pendennis Castle three miles from Penrhyn in the autumn of 1595.

But more permanently persuasive than these anecdotes and pertinent even to the stage of to-day are two other of Heywood's pleas. The first is the international attraction of London as a theatrical centre, " playing is an ornament to the city, which strangers of all nations repairing hither report of in their countries, beholding them here with some admiration ; for what variety of entertainment can there be in any city of Christendom more than in London ?"

The second is the beneficial influence of the stage on English speech and versification.

> Our English tongue which hath been the most harsh, uneven and broken language of the world, part Dutch, part Irish, Saxon, Scotch, Welsh and indeed a gallimafry (hotch-potch) of many, but perfect in none is now by this secondary means of playing, continually refined, every writer striving in himself to add a new flourish unto it, so that in process from the most rude and unpolished tongue, it is grown to a most perfect and composed language.

The *Apology*, like so much of Heywood's work, is

deficient in orderly arrangement, but it is effective because it is the fruit of experience and conviction, and because Heywood is more concerned to present his own case than to indulge in abuse of his opponents. The pamphlet when printed well deserved the verse commendations in notably affectionate terms from John Webster to his beloved friend and from the actors Richard Perkins, Christopher Beeston, Robert Pallant and John Taylor to their good friend and fellow.

The best proof of the success of the pamphlet is that it provoked in 1615 a railing reply *A Refutation of the Apology for Actors* by J. G. ; and that it was republished at an uncertain date during the Commonwealth by William Cartwright, as *The Actors' Vindication* with a most inaccurate dedication to the Marquess of Dorchester and other unauthorised alterations. That in our own day it has an enduring value in more senses than one is testified by the fact that in 1948 I received a catalogue from Quaritch in which a copy of the original edition was offered for sale at £100.

CHAPTER 7

The Four Ages : Golden, Silver, Brazen, Iron

In *Troia Britannica* Heywood had found in classical
mythology the materials for a narrative poem. On the
same inexhaustible source he was afterwards to draw
for a comprehensive dramatic series, *The Golden Age*
(1611), *The Silver Age* (1612), *The Brazen Age* (1613) and
The Iron Age, in two parts (1632).

Dr. Clark has claimed that the four *Ages* are all
dramatisations of *Troia Britannica,* but in the *Journal of
English and Germanic Philology,* October, 1946, Mr. Alan
Holaday has argued that this is only true of the *Golden*
and portions of the other three, and that the *Silver* and
the *Brazen* especially contain references to properties
listed by Henslowe as used in two 1595 *Hercules* plays.
It seems therefore that F. G. Fleay was partly right in
his view that the *Ages* were revised versions of plays
acted by the Lord Admiral's men.

In any case it is somewhat surprising that these
mythological subjects should have been a " draw " at
popular theatres. But the title-page of *The Golden Age*
speaks of it as " sundry times acted at the Red Bull by
the Queen's Majesty's servants," and in his preface
Heywood claims that it hath " passed the approbation
of auditors." In the " preface to the reader " of *The
Iron Age* he asserts that " these were the plays often (and
not with the least applause) publicly acted by two
companies upon one stage at once, and have at sundry
times thronged three several theatres with numerous

and nightly auditories." In disagreement with Dr. Clark and Quincy Adams I think that these words refer only to *The Iron Age* pieces and not to all the *Ages*. Two of the theatres appear to have been the Red Bull and the Curtain, the third is doubtful. In any case we know from the Revels accounts that *The Silver Age* and *The Rape of Lucrece* were performed by the King's and Queen's Companies before Queen Anne and Prince Henry at Greenwich on 12th and 13th January, 1611–12.

Heywood gained his success by adroitly mingling with the more serious and unfamiliar features of his mythological and legendary themes lighter and spectacular elements and he carries the whole series through with his characteristic unflagging gusto. He brings on Homer to speak a prologue to each of the first three *Ages*.

> I was the man
> That flourish'd in the world's first infancy :
> When it was young and knew not how to speak,
> I taught it speech and understanding both
> Even in the cradle . . .
> I was the Muses' patron, Learning's spring,
> And you shall once more hear blind Homer sing.

It was, however, much later " singers " than Homer who supplied tunes for Heywood's *Ages*.

The Golden Age in his presentation of it here is far from being, as ordinarily conceived, a peaceful one. It dramatises the conflict between Saturn and his brother Titan, and the latter's attempt to secure succession to supreme sovereignty ; the escape of Jupiter from being murdered at birth, his growth in disguise to manhood and his amours with Calisto and Danae. And what probably was the main attraction to his theatrical audiences was the series of battles with " alarms, drums, colours and soldiers," first between Saturn and Titan with his sons, then between Jupiter and the Titan brood, and finally between Jupiter and his father Saturn whose crown he seizes. This has hitherto been only the crown of Crete, but now " by virtue of divinest poesy," Jupiter and his brothers, Neptune and Pluto become immortal Gods. In the dumb show with which *The Golden Age* closes the three Fates place in a globe three lots, of which Jupiter draws heaven, to which he ascends on an eagle, Neptune the sea, and is mounted on a sea-horse, Pluto hell, for which he is arrayed in a burning robe and crown.

In Act I of *The Silver Age* Heywood carries on the story of Acrisius, the father of Danae, deposed by his brother Pretus for his cruelty towards her ; delivered by Danae's son Perseus (accompanied by Andromeda rescued from the sea-monster) whom Acrisius creates king and queen of Argos.

But it is in Act II that Heywood shows, though in miniature, his true dramatic quality. His *flair* for handling domestic situations finds congenial scope in the episode of Jupiter's amour with Alcmena, in the disguise of her husband Amphitrio (as the name is here spelt) who is on active service, with Ganymede impersonating the servant Sosia. To the Plautine plot Heywood adds details of his own. When Jupiter, to prolong his dalliance with Alcmena, bids three nights be put into one, he declares :

The Antipodes to us shall have a day
Of three days' length. Now at this hour is fought
By Joshua, Duke unto the Hebrew nation,
(Who are indeed the Antipodes to us)

His famous battle 'gainst the Canaanites,
And at his orison the sun stands still
That he may have their slaughter.

It is one of the most surprising of Heywood's efforts to synchronise mythology with Scripture.

After Jupiter has been entertained by Alcmena and has related to her the victory won by Amphitrio, the real Sosia knocks at the gate to announce his master's return, and is denied admission by his counterfeit who beats him. Sosia's bewilderment finds subtle expression :

Sosia.   I am Sosia, you may strike if you will but in beating me (if you be Sosia) I assure you, you shall but beat yourself.
Gan.   The fellow's mad.
Sosia.   Mad ! am I not newly landed ? Sent hither by my master ? Is not this our house ? Do I not speak ? Am I not awake ? Am I not newly beaten ? Do I not feel it still ? And shall I doubt I am not myself ?

His confusion becomes intensified when Ganymede gives him a true account of his recent doings, and he cries despairingly.

Somebody for charity sake either lend or give me a name, for this I have lost by the way, and now I look better on he, me ; or I, he : as he hath got my name, he hath got my shape, countenance, stature, and every thing so right, that he can be no other than I myself . . . where have I miscarried ? Where been changed ? Did I not leave myself behind in the ship when I came away ? . . . Farewell self !

He hurries off with his strange tale to Amphitrio
who dismisses it as " most deeply incredible." But
when he triumphantly greets his wife, he is amazed to
find that she thinks he is flouting her by repeating what
he had just told her during the night. She is roused to
protest :

> Shall I be plain, my lord ? I take it ill
> That you, whom I receiv'd late yester night,
> Gave you my freest welcome, feasted you,
> Lodg'd you, and but this morning, two hours since,
> Took leave of you with tears, that your return,
> So sudden, should be furnisht with such scorn.

Amphitrio exclaims :

> Gentlemen, I fear the madness of my man
> Is fled into her brain.

He calls his captains to witness that he is but newly
landed, while Alcmena's servants testify that they
waited on her and her husband at a midnight banquet.
When he flings the taunt of " strumpet " in her face,
she retorts :

> Your jealousy
> And this imposterous wrong heaps on me
> injuries
> More than my sex can bear : you had best
> deny
> The gift you gave me too.

Amph. O heaven ! what gift ?
Alc. The golden cup the Theleboans' King
Us'd still to quaff in.
Amph. Indeed I had such purpose,
But that I keep safe lock't. Show me the
bowl.

Amphitrio thus plays what he feels sure is a trump card, not knowing that Mercury has stolen the bowl out of its casket for Jupiter who has given it to Alcmena. He cannot believe his eyes when she hands it to him, and he bids Sosia fetch it from the casket. Well may the servant exclaim :

> This is the strangest that ere I heard. I, Sosia, have begot another Sosia, my Lord Amphitrio hath begot another Amphitrio. Now if this golden bowl have begot another golden bowl, we shall all be twinnet and doubled.

With the reappearance of the disguised Jupiter there are further complications till even Amphitrio is forced to doubt his own and his servant's identities.

Amph. What art thou ?
Sos. Nay, what art thou ?
Amph. I am not myself.
Sos. You would not believe me when I said I was not myself. Why should I believe you ?
Amph. Art thou Sosia ?
Sos. That's more than I can resolve you, for the world is grown so dangerous, a man dares scarce make bold with his own name ; but I am he that was sent with a letter to my lady.
Amph. And I am he that sent thee with this letter. Yet dare not say I am Amphitrio :
My wife, house, friends, my servants all deny me.
Sos. You have reason to love me the better since none sticks to you but I.

Then suddenly a wellnigh tragic note is struck as Amphitrio appeals to the heavens to fall upon him, or eternal sleep to cast a film before his eyes,

That they may ne'er more gaze upon yon heavens
That have beheld my shame : or sleep, or death,
Command me shut these optic windows in.
     . . . be my pillow, Sosia.
For I must sleep.

The tension is relieved as Sosia turns to the audience
and begs them " make no noise for waking me or my
master." While they sleep Juno, attended by Iris,
descends to have revenge upon her faithless spouse and
his paramour. But she is forestalled by Jupiter who,
after thunder and lightning, " appears in his glory under
a rainbow, to whom they all kneel." He bids Amphitrio, to whom he has given victory in war, make peace
with Alcmena, " she that never bosom'd mortal save
thee." Amphitrio humbly obeys :

Jove is our patron, and his power our awe ;
His majesty our wonder : will, our law.

The fruit of Jupiter's amour with Alcmena is Hercules
and the scenes that follow present his earlier labours
culminating in his descent into Hell to rescue Proserpine whom Pluto has borne down to be his Queen.
The pyrotechnic resources of the playhouse must have
been severely taxed by the stage directions that follow :

Hercules sinks himself. Flashes of fire : the Devils
appear at every corner of the stage with several fireworks. The Judges of Hell and the three Sisters move
over the stage Hercules after them. Fireworks all
over the house. Enter Hercules . . . Enter Pluto with
a club of fire, a burning crown ; Proserpine, the
Judges, the Fates, and a guard of Devils, all with
burning weapons . . . Hercules fells Pluto, beats off
the Devils, with all their fireworks, rescues Proserpine.

All the ghosts join with Proserpine in applause :

> Long live eterniz'd noble Hercules
> That hath dissolv'd our torments !

But Rhadamanthus calls a halt :

> I charge thee stir not hence
> Till we have censur'd* thee and Proserpine.
> Is not the power of Jove confin'd above ?
> And are not we as absolute in state
> Here in the vaults below ? To alter this
> The heavens must fail, the sun melt in his heat,
> The elements dissolve, Chaos again
> Confuse the triple mass, all turn to nothing.
> Now there is order : Gods there are and Devils :
> These reward virtue : the others punish vice,
> Alter this course, you mingle bad with good.

It is a striking expression of the dominant Elizabethan view of the necessity for " order " or " degree " in all things, and Hercules cries approvingly " Rhadamanth speaks well." He then appeals to the planetary gods for judgment, and they " take their places as they are in height." There is a lively debate till Rhadamanthus declares :

> If since her first arrive
> She hath tasted any food, she must of force
> Be everlastingly confin'd to Hell.

A witness deposes that she has eaten some few grains of a pomegranate, and the gods cry : " She must be Pluto's." Her mother Ceres, appeals to Jupiter :

> Justice, oh justice, thou Omnipotent,
> Rob not thy Ceres of her beauteous child.
> Either restore my daughter to the earth,
> Or banish me to Hell.

*Judged.

Jupiter, identifying Proserpine with the Moon, gives
a solemn verdict, arbitrating impartially between both
parties :

> We have not, O you Gods,
> Purpose to do our Stygian brother wrong,
> Nor rob the heavens the Planet of the Moon
> By whom the seas are sway'd. Be she confin'd
> Below the earth, where be the ebbs and tides ?
> Where is her power infus'd in herbs and plants ?

> *   *   *   *   *

> the year we part in twelve,
> Call'd months of the moon : twelve times a year
> She in full splendour shall supply her orb,
> And shine in heaven : twelve times fill Pluto's
> arms
> Below in Hell . . . Parted so even,
> We neither favour Hell, nor gloze with Heaven.

All acclaim the award, and among the many trial
scenes on the Elizabethan stage this has its distinctive
place.

The Brazen Age dramatises the later labours of Hercules and connects loosely with them a variety of episodes. In the hunt of the Calydonian boar Adonis is
wounded to death, Meleager triumphs but, handing
the spoil of victory to the maiden Atalanta, suffers his
predestined death when his mother throws on the fire
the fatal brand. There follows the quest of the Argonauts for the Golden Fleece, with the sudden passion
of the enchantress Medea for Jason and her resolve that
he shall succeed by her aid in his perilous enterprise.

> I that by incantations can remove
> Hills from their sites, and make huge mountains
> shake,
> Darken the sun at noon, call from their graves

> Ghosts long since dead ; that can command the
>   earth,
> And affright heaven, no spell at all can find
> To bondage love, or free a captive mind.

And again this stage direction must have taxed the resources of a Stuart playhouse.

> Two fiery bulls are discovered, the fleece hanging over them and the dragon sleeping beneath them : Medea with strange fireworks hangs above in the air in the strange habit of a conjuress !

Then after the tragic close of the Argonauts' story, not to cloy the appetites (as Homer announces) of the " courteous auditors . . . with viands of one table," Heywood switches the action to the amour of Mars and Venus with its humorous sequel. The episode is adroitly turned to stage purposes. The servant Gallus is bidden awake them before the sun rises but oversleeps and is changed into a cock who henceforth will always crow to proclaim the sun's coming. Meanwhile Aurora enters attended by the Seasons, Days and Hours, and is saluted by Phoebus before he begins his daily round.

> We with this eye
> Can all things see that mortals do on earth
> And what we find inhuman, or to offend,
> We tell to Jove that he may punish sins.
> For this I'm term'd a tell-tale and a blab,
> And that I nothing can conceal abroad.

He at once espies Mars and Venus in each other's arms and tells Vulcan who catches them in a draw-net, and calls all the Gods, who " appear above and laugh " at the sinners till Vulcan releases them.

With the last Act Hercules reappears, captive to the charms of the Lydian queen, Omphale, attired like a woman with a distaff and a spindle. A band of Greek heroes come to seek him with gifts from his deserted wife Deianira, and cannot believe their eyes when they see him kissing Omphale's foot.

Pollux. Lady, our purpose was to Hercules,
Show us the man.
Omph. Behold him, Greeks, there.
Abreus. Where?
Omph. There at his task.
Jason. Alas! This Hercules!
This is some base effeminate groom, not he
That with his puissance frighted all the earth,
This is some woman, some Hermaphrodite.

They recite the mighty deeds of that noble Hercules till Jason announces:

To him we came, but since he lives not here,
Come, lords, we will return these presents back
Unto the constant lady, whence they came.

Then at last Hercules is stirred into self-recall.

Did we all this? where is that spirit become
That was in us? no marvel, Hercules,
If thou beest strange to them that thus disguis'd
Art to thyself unknown. Hence with that distaff
And base effeminate chores!*

In vain Omphale seeks to keep him in submission, and when he asks " who spake? " Jason answers:

Think that was Deianira's voice,
That calls thee home to dry her widowed tears,
And to bring comfort to her desolate bed.

*Household jobs.

In proof of his re-transformation Hercules declares :

> This day unto the Gods I'll sacrifice,
> To grace which pomp, and that we may appear
> The same we were before us shall be borne
> These of our labours twelve . . .
> Whilst we upon our manly shoulders bear
> These massy pillars we in Gades must rear.

Then follows another of the detailed stage directions :

> Enter to the sacrifice two priests to the altar, six
> princes with six of his labours, in the midst Hercules
> bearing his two brazen pillars, six other princes with
> the other six labours.

As they march over the stage the servant Lichas
appears with Deianira's gift, the shirt stained with the
blood of the centaur Nessus, supposed to be a love
charm, but in reality fatal to its wearer. The action
that follows, with its sacrificial background, and its
gradual ascent to its terrific climax is masterly in its
stagecraft. As Hercules puts on the shirt he declares :

> With this her present I put on her love :
> Witness heaven, earth, and all you Peers of Greece,
> I wed her once more in this ornament,
>   *   *   *   *   *
> So now before Jove's altar let us kneel
> And make our peace with heaven.

As the princes kneel at the altar, the sacrificing priest in
a fine image bids them join their prayers with his,

> For mortal orisons are sons to Jove,
> And, when none else can, they have free access
> Unto their father's ear.

His solemn invocation is interrupted by the first cry of agony from Hercules, and the command " no more ! " But the hero seeks to control his anguish and bids the priest proceed till the inner torment becomes unbearable, and in mad fury he kills the innocent messenger Lichas and Omphale, unexpectedly faithful in his extremity, whom he takes to be Deianira. Then resolved to die by his own hand he bids the princes raise and set alight a funeral pyre of trees, into which he leaps and burns his club and lion's skin, " which none but he can wield." And with a last proud farewell he cries to his peers :

Heap fire on fire.
And pile on pile, till you have made a structure
To flame as high as heaven, and record this,
Though by the Gods and Fates we are o'er-thrown,
Alcides dies by no hand but his own.

With a transformation scene *The Brazen Age* closes.

Jupiter above strikes him with a thunderbolt, his body sinks, and from the heavens descends a hand in a cloud, that from the place where Hercules was burnt brings up a star, and fixeth it in the firmament.

With *The Iron Age* Heywood passes from mythology to the legendary tale of Troy. Paris is about to set sail to Greece to seek requital for the rape of Priam's sister Hesione by carrying off the beauteous Spartan queen. Two women in vain raise their voices against his plan. His sister Cassandra " with her hair about her ears " is a prophetess of the woe to come.

Stay this bold youth, my brother, who by water
Would sail to bring fire which shall burn all Troy.
Stay him, oh, stay him, ere these golden roofs
Melt o'er our heads, these glorious turrets
Be burnt to ashes.

And the forsaken Œnone, having seen the cedars of
Mount Ida hewn down,

to build a fleet

> For Paris, who in that must sail to Greece
> To fetch a new wife thence,

appeals to him to stay, only to be told,

> Hark, hark ! the sailors cry, " aboard, aboard ! "
> The wind blows fair, farewell !

When the Trojans reach Sparta, Menclaus welcomes
them, embracing Paris and the rest, but Paris turns
and kisses Helen, " allway she with her hand puts him
back," protesting,

> 'Tis not the Spartan fashion thus to greet
> Upon the lips, when royal strangers meet.
> I know not what your Asian courtship is :

but adding aside, " O Jove, how sweetly doth this
Trojan kiss." And when they are left alone together
again she murmurs to herself :

> O kiss me, if thou lov'st me, once again !
> I feel the first kiss thrill through every vein.

> *Paris.* Queen, I must speak with you.
> *Helen.*   Must ?
> *Paris.*   Helen, aye.
>   I have but two ways to take, to speak or die.

*   *   *   *   *

> O Jove, think I had now an angel's voice,
> As you an angel's shape have, that my words
> Might sound as sphere-like music in your ear !
> That Jove himself, whom I must call to witness,
> Would now stand forth in person to approve
> What I now speak : Helen, Helen, I love ;
> Chide me, I care not ; tell your husband, do.

Queen Elizabeth, with Crown and Sceptre, in *The Exemplary Lives of Nine the Most Worthy Women of the World.*

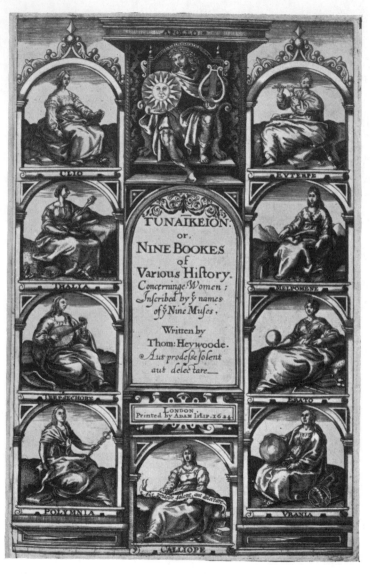

Title page of Γυναικεῖον, with Apollo and the Nine Muses.

Fearless of death, behold, I boldly woo.
For let me live bright Helen to enjoy,
Or let me never back re-sail to Troy.

To this rapturous outburst Helen makes coy re-
sponses till the unsuspecting Menclaus re-enters to
entertain his visitors at a banquet which, with the
drinking of healths all round, must have made a gay
stage spectacle, though with the undertone of the
cynical comments of Thersites. Then in a curious
episode Paris suddenly feigns to be ill and to fall into
a sleep from which, when Menclaus (bound on a
mission to Crete) and the others have departed, he
starts up to renew, with an adroit variation, his
amorous pleading.

Your husband left me charge I should enjoy
All that the Court can yield : if all, then you.
I would not for the world but you should do
All that the King, your lord, commands you to,

She replies in a similar strain :

Do not I blush, sweet stranger ? if I break
The laws of modesty, think that I speak
But with my husband's tongue, for I say still
I would not yield but to obey his will.

All that remains is to agree on a plot by which Helen
will be brought, apparently by force, on board Paris's
ship, which will " hoist up sail, ne'er to return again."
  With Act II the scene shifts to Troy, with the two
armies face to face and after " a great alarum and ex-
cursions," with heavy slaughter on both sides, Hector
steps between them holding up his lance. In medieval,
not classical, fashion, he casts down his gauntlet to
challenge any Grecian Knight to single combat. When

Ajax, Achilles, and Diomede vie to take it up, Ajax is
chosen by lot and meets Hector in a duel in which,
after both have lost their swords and shields, Hector
casts a great piece of rock at Ajax, who retorts by
assailing Hector with a tree he has torn up by the roots.
From such abnormal combat they are parted by both
armies, and a truce is proclaimed during which Priam
invites twenty of the Greek princes to a banquet in his
palace.

This banquet, graced with loud music, and with
Trojans and Greeks sitting side by side at a long table,
is the counterpart, as Paris tactlessly reminds Menelaus,
of that at Sparta, at which the flight of Helen was devised. Well may Menelaus retort,

> But that these tongues
> Should be as well truce bound as our sharp weapons,
> We could be bitter, Paris, but have done.

Then in a succession of short, staccato speeches Heywood skilfully presents the different groups, each with
its own pre-occupations. Achilles declares himself
subdued by the charms of Priam's daughter Polyxena,
Calchas is whispering to his daughter Cressida to fly
from Troilus and doomed Troy to the arms of the
Grecian King Diomede. Troilus gives Diomede the
lie for declaring that he unhorsed him in fight, and
there is a general strife of tongues till Agamemnon
calms it and bids his fellow Kings

> Pledge me King Priam in a cupfull crown'd,

The drinking of the toast is followed by a "lofty
dance of sixteen princes, half Trojans, half Grecians,"
but harmony is again broken by a proposal by Achilles.
Prompted by his sudden passion for Polyxena he is

anxious for the war to end, and for the Greeks to leave Troy with honour. He urges that Helen, cause of all the strife, should be set between Menclaus and Paris, and that whichever of them she chooses shall enjoy her still. In an effective scene the two rivals make their appeal, with Helen irresolute between them, till at last she decides, first looking at Menclaus,

That way I should because I know 'tis meeter,

and then turning otherwards,

But I'll this way for Paris kisses sweeter.

Whereupon Menclaus cries " Grecians to arms ! " There follow the alarums, the detached episodes of fighting so popular with Tudor and Stuart audiences in which, with Achilles idle in his tent, the Trojans have the upper hand till the death of Patroclus at Hector's hand, and the taunts of Ajax bring Achilles again into the field. With Heywood's *flair* for domestic pathos he elaborates the scene in which Hector's kith and kin, led by Andromache, beseech him not to fight on an ill-omened day.

And.   My dearest love,
         Pity your wife, your son, your father : all
         These live beneath the safeguard of that
         arm.

          *   *   *   *   *

Priam.   If thou fall
         Who then shall stand ? Troy shall consume
         with fire,
         Therefore, dear Hector, cast they armour
         off.
And.   Husband !
Hector. Son !

Helen.   Brother !
Hector.   By Jove. I am resolved.
And.   Oh, all ye gods !
Hector.   Not all the devils,
            Could half torment me like these women's
            tongues.

But at last Paris prevails with him to leave fighting
that day to his brothers, till standing on the walls he
sees the youthful Margareton killed by Achilles, and
he leaps down with the cry "'Tis none but Hector must
revenge his death."

After spreading havoc through the Grecian host, he
sends his javelin quivering through the thigh of
Achilles who does not meet him in fair fight but calls
to his bodyguard of Myrmidons.

                    your steel poleaxes
Fix all at once and girt him round with wounds.

Well may Hector exclaim :

Dishonourable Greek, Hector ne'er dealt
On base advantage, or ever lift his sword
Over a quaking foe, but as a spoil
Unworthy us still left him to his fear :
Nor on the man, whom singly I struck down,
Have I redoubled blows ; my valour still
Opposed against a standing enemy
Thee have I twice unhorsed, and when I might
Have slain thee grovelling left thee to the field.

Thus the Trojan *chevalier sans peur et sans reproche* meets
an unseemly end through treachery.   His brother
Troilus, who in *The Iron Age* figures more as a warrior
than a lover, vows revenge :

They call him Hector's ghost, he glides so quick
through our battalions

So Ulysses tauntingly tells Achilles who sends Troilus to his doom as he had done Hector. But treachery is a game at which more than one can play, and Achilles by the bait of Polyxena is lured to Priam's palace where Paris fatally wounds him with an arrow in his only vulnerable part, his heel. There is a short fifth Act of anti-climax where the armour of Achilles is awarded to Ulysses in preference to Ajax, who stung by this ignominy and by the gibes of Thersites takes his own life. It is left to Thersites in an epilogue, in the spirit of Falstaff after Shrewsbury fight, after reciting the fate of heroes on both sides, to point the moral to the audience :

> All these brave ones die.
> Ha ! ha ! judge you : Is it not better far
> To keep ourselves in breath, and linger war ?

The first three Acts of *The Second Part of the Iron Age* presents the fall of Troy, with the bloodthirsty Pyrrhus, raging to avenge the death of his father Achilles as the central figure. Heywood mainly follows the *Aeneid*, Book II, from which five lines in the original Latin are spoken by Hector's ghost. But the stately Virgilian narrative undergoes a crudely melodramatic dramatisation, culminating in the massacre, before the altar, of Priam and his family, with the stage direction, " They are all slain at once," and the perjured Sinon's exultant cry, " Why, so, so, this was stately tragical ! "

With the fourth Act the scene shifts to Mycenæ where Clytemnestra with her paramour Aegisthus and her children, Orestes and Electra, and Hermione, daughter of Menelaus and Helen, greet Agamemnon on his victorious return. In the scene of his treacherous murder Heywood again displays his finer dramatic power. As Agamemnon and his queen make ready for

bed the former talks light-heartedly and gratefully
about the progress made by Orestes and Electra during
his absence. Suddenly he starts, as if hearing someone,
and casts suspicious glances round the chamber ; even
the bed has for him a sinister touch and look.

Aga.	How hard this down feels ! like a monument
	Cut out of marble. Beds resemble graves,
	And these, methinks, appear like winding sheets
	Prepar'd for corses.
Cly.	O how ominously
	Do you presage : you much affright me, sir,
	In this our long-wished meeting.
Aga.	All's shook off :
	Now I am arm'd for pleasure: you commended
	Late one Aegisthus to me ; prithee, Queen,
	Of what condition is he ?

And Aegisthus, concealed behind the bed-curtains,
leaps forth with sword drawn, to give the answer,
" Tyrant, this," echoed by Clytemnestra, " And I am
thus his second." The King falls dying beneath their
attack, while, " a great thunder crack " proclaims to
the world a monarch's fall by treason.

The Greek dramatists represent the revenge of
Orestes for his father's murder as a delayed action, but
Heywood foreshortens the event, and in Act V Orestes
frustrates a design of Aegisthus on his own life by killing
him. Clytemnestra asserts :

I am as innocent of that black deed
As was this guiltless gentleman here dead.

Orestes invokes a sign from Heaven or Hell, and the
ghost of Agamemnon enters pointing to his wounds and

then to Aegisthus and the queen. Had Heywood in mind in what follows the closet-scene between Hamlet and his mother ? In any case there is at first a parallelism, though the outcome is different.

Orest.	Godlike shape,
	Have you, my father, left the Elyzium fields,
	Where all the ancient heroes live in bliss,
	To bring yourself this sacred testimony
	To crown my approbation—Lady, see !
Cly.	See what ? thy former murder makes thee mad.
Orest.	Rest, Ghost, in peace ! I now am justified
	And need no further witness ; saw you nothing ?
Cly.	What should I see, but this sad spectacle,
	Which blood-shoots both mine eyes ?
Orest.	And nothing else ?
Cly.	Nothing.
Orest.	Mine eyes are clearer sighted then, and see
	Into thy bosom. Murderess !

   *   *   *   *   *

being a wife and Queen,
Thou killd'st a King and husband, and hast taught,
Me, being a son, how to destroy a mother.

But Orestes has not only his father's murder to avenge. His beloved Hermione has been betrothed by her father to Pyrrhus, who at this unseasonable hour is wedding her at the altar when Orestes rushes in with sword drawn and crying :

Priam before the holy altar fell :
Before the altar bid thy life farewell.
Rescue Hermione !

In the confused fight that follows Orestes and Pyrrhus kill each other and of the protagonists Ulysses alone survives, bearing in his arms Hermione from whom her mother Helen takes a looking glass and laments :

> Where is that beauty ? Lives it in this face,
> Which hath set two parts of the world at war,
> Been ruin of the Asian monarchy,
> And almost this of Europe ? this the beauty,
> That lauch'd a thousand ships from Anlis gulf,
> In such a poor repurchase, now decayed ?

And unable to bear the contrast of herself with the Helen of whose idealisation by Marlowe there is here an echo she takes her own life.

Ulysses as " the man solely reserv'd' appears to speak the author's epilogue :

> If he have been too bloody, 'tis the story.
> Truth claims excuse, and seeks no further glory,
> Or if you think he hath done your patience wrong
> In tedious scenes, by keeping you so long,
> Much matter in few words, he bade me say,
> Are hard to express ; that lengthened out his play.

CHAPTER 8

Γυναικεῖον *or* The History of Women—The Exemplary
Lives

In 1624 Heywood returned to prose composition
(mixed with some translated verse) in Γυναικεῖον, or
Nine Books of Various History Concerning Women. It
was printed by Adam Islip and was dedicated to the
Earl of Worcester, as the appropriate patron of good
women, having been " the happy husband and fortunate father of such." The work is a folio of 466 pages
in nine books and after the precedent of Herodotus in-
scribed by the names of one of the nine Muses, each of
whom is pictured separately in the engraved title-page.

As the reference to good women in the dedication to
the Earl of Worcester implies, the work, though it includes the histories of a number of infamous women, is
in the main an Apology for their sex. And like the
Apology for Actors it is a contribution to a long-standing
controversy which had been embittered by the publication in 1615 of Joseph Swetnam's pamphlet, *The
Arraignment of Lewd, idle, forward and inconstant Women*.
This had a remarkable success and ran through one
edition after another. Heywood had doubtless Swetnam and his fellow travellers in mind when in the prefatory address to the Reader he declares :

I have exposed to thy most judicial view a discourse of women, wherein expect not that I should
either enviously carp at the particular manners or

actions of any living or ingeniously detract from the sepulchres of the dead ; the first I could never affect ; the last I did always detest.

Γυναικεῖον is as comprehensive, and as unmethodical in detail, as *Troia Britannica*. Book I is concerned with Goddesses and ends with an abstract in verse of all the fables in the fifteen books of Ovid's *Metamorphoses*. Book II introduces Muses, Sybils, Graces, and other mythological or legendary damsels. Book III passes to more earthly representatives of their sex. It treats of Illustrious Queens, Famous Wives, Mothers, Daughters etc. It begins with a discussion of how far drinking or kissing was permissible to women of good repute. Heywood quotes the view of Cato that " the use of kissing first begun betwixt kinsmen and kinswomen, howsoever near allied or far off, only by that to know whether their wives, daughters, or nieces had tasted any wine." He then makes an interesting confession of his own opinion (p. 118).

But kissing and drinking both are now grown (it seems) to a greater custom amongst us than in those days with the Romans : nor am I so austere to forbid the use of either, both which, the one in surfeits, the other in adulteries, may be abused by the vicious, yet contrarily at customary meetings and laudable banquets, they by the nobly disposed, and such whose hearts are fixed upon honour, may be used with much modesty and continence.

Thereupon he adds a statement that he has no didactic aim in his volume.

But the purpose of my tractate is to exemplify, not to instruct ; to show you precedents of virtue from others, not to fashion any new imaginary form from

myself ; and that setting so many statues of honour
before your eyes, of beauty, nobleness, magnanimity,
bounty, courtesy, temperance, and whatsoever else
in goodness can be included, each heroic and well
disposed lady, or woman lower degreed and under-
qualified, may out of all, or some of these at least,
apprehend some one thing or other worthy imitation.

He then declares that no man was ever known to be
eminent whom woman in some manner hath not
equalled, and gives illustrations from classical legend
and history, in particular Alcestis. Among illustrious
queens he mentions a number of old-world figures,
including Semiramis, Cleopatra and Zenobia. From
them he turns with characteristic abruptness to those
of his own time and country (p. 123).

Amongst whom let me not be so unnatural to her
merit, or so ungrateful to my country (thrice blest
and divinely happy in her most fortunate reign) as
not to remember that ever to be celebrated Princess,
Elizabeth of late memory, Queen of England . . .
of whose omniscience, pantarite* and goodness
all men heretofore have spoke to little ; no man
hereafter can write too much ; sacred be still her
memory to us on earth, as her blessed soul lives ever
glorified in heaven.

Of all Heywood's tributes to Elizabeth this, written
twenty-one years after death, is the most reverentially
fervent, and does honour alike to his loyalty to her
memory and to the transcendent impression of her
personality even from the grave. In a somewhat lower
key but equally unqualified in its praise is his tribute

* This word is not in the *Oxford English Dictionary*, and, if not a misprint, its meaning is doubtful.

to another deceased queen, Anne of Denmark, wife of James I, who had died in 1619.

> Her succeeded (though not in her absolute monarchy) yet a Princess of unspotted fame, incomparable clemency, unmatchable goodness, and most remarkable virtue, Queen Anne whom all degrees honoured, all nations loved, and no tongue was ever heard to asperse with the least calumny ; who in her too short eminence here amongst us was known to be the step of dignity to many, but detriment to none, in whom all were glad, by whom none had ever the least cause of sorrow, unless in the lamented loss of so grave and gracious a princess.

To this Heywood adds a " few funeral tears upon her hearse " in the form of an Ode of eleven seven-lined stanzas. And in what he calls this " catalogue of Queens " he passes from Anne to her daughter, Elizabeth, whose wedding to Frederick, King of Bohemia, had been celebrated with such pomp and rejoicing in 1613, who was now a fugitive from her capital, but had borne herself with courage and dignity.

> To who I must give that attribute which all soldiers bestow upon her, *The Queen of women and the best of Queens*, whose magnanimity in war, and gentleness in peace, resolution in the one, and generous affability in the other, have so sweet a correspondence that when the cannon roared loud at the gates, and the bullet forced a passage even through the palace where she lodged, was no more daunted in courage nor dismayed in countenance than when the gentle and soft music melodiously sounded at the celebration of her espousals.

Heywood then returns to the celebration of a long series of legendary illustrious women, after which in what he is bold enough to claim is " no ridiculous digression," he proceeds to " wonder how the name of cuckold came to be so frequent among us." And in this connection he introduces one of the best of the short stories which are the most attractive feature of Γυναικεῖον.

There was a disputation in Hell as to what a cuckold was as every one examined by Lucifer denied being the same. It was decided to send one of the most ingenious devils to earth " to discover this strange unknown creature, and if it were possible to bring him thither alive." By a complicated series of happenings the emissary brings back, thinking it to be a cuckold, a bear-baiting mastiff in a sack to where Lucifer is seated in state, with his princes, judges and officers about him, expecting the much desired object (p. 159).

The sack's mouth is opened, out flies the mastiff amongst them who, seeing so many ugly creatures together, thought (it seems) he had been amongst the bears in Paris-garden, but spying Lucifer to be the greatest and most ill-favoured amongst them, first leaps up into his face, and after flies at whomsoever stood next him. The devils are dispersed, everyone runs and makes what shift he can for himself ; the sessions is dissolved, the bench and bale-dock cleared, and all in general so affrighted that ever since that accident the very name hath been so terrible amongst them, as they had rather entertain into their dark and sad dominions ten thousand of their wives than any one man who bear's the least character of a cuckold !

Heywood opens the fourth book, " Of women in-
cestuous, of adulteresses, and such as have come by
strange deaths " with a plea for exculpation (p. 163).

Never did my hand more compulsively direct my
pen, nor my pen with less willingness blot paper than
at this present, being fixed in this tractate to lay
open the frailties of this sex, before so much commended. But this is my encouragement to proceed,
because I can produce nothing out of history to the
disgrace of the bad and vicious, which adds not to
the honour of the good and virtuous. Were none
foul, what benefit were to be fair ? and if none de-
formed, what grace could it be to be well featured ?

To this somewhat disingenuous argument he appends
a truly astonishing one :

And as it hath pleased the divine providence to
provide a heaven and a hell, the one to crown the
virtuous, the other to condemn the wicked ; so there
is a necessity of number to people both, nor are the
torments of the one more feelingly apprehended than
in contemplating the joys and felicities of the other.

It is predestined that there must be enough sinners to
prevent there being a vacuum in hell !

There follows among Heywood's examples of adulteresses what he calls a " modern history," within his
own knowledge, of a young gentlewoman married to
an elderly gentleman and of her conduct to two lovers.
This story, as has been seen,* was used by Heywood as
the main plot of his play *The English Traveller*.

Book V treats first of the Amazons and other legendary figures and then passes to warlike women of a

*See page 45.

more historic type. Of Joan of Arc Heywood, it is to
be noted, gives an objectively equitable account, without any of the prejudice patent in the play, *King Henry
VI, Part I.* After telling of her victories, her capture,
and her execution in the market place of Rouen, he
ends : (p. 239)

> Twenty-six years after Charles the King for a
> great sum of money procured an annihilation of the
> first sentence from the Pope in which she was pro-
> claimed a virago* inspired with divine instinct ; in
> memory of whose virtuous life and unjust death he
> caused a fair cross to be erected first in the place
> where her body was burned.

Of English martial heroines he singles out the empress
Maud, the wife of King Stephen, Emma, wife of King
Ethelred, and Margaret, queen of King Henry VI.

Passing from valiant to fair or beautiful women
Heywood seems to forget his promise not to be didactic
and warns the sex that Nature in various forms out-
rivals their beauties (p. 241).

> You that are proud of your hair behold the feathers
> of the jay or parrot, with the admirable variety of
> the pheasant and peacock. What rose in the cheek
> can countervail the rose of the garden ? Or what
> azure vein in the temples the blue flower of the field ?
> Come to outward habit or ornament, what woman
> doth better become the richest attire (though fetched
> from the farthest parts of the world) than the panther
> his stains and the leopard his pleasing and delightful
> spots ? Are not the fishes as beautiful in their silver
> shining scales, and the terrible dragon as glorious in
> his golden armour as woman apparelled in cloth of

*Virgin.

bodkin or tissue. Where is she that exceeds the dove or swan in whiteness or the pine or cedar in straightness ? Let me hear her voice that can compare with the nightingale in sweetness, or behold the eye that can look upon the sun with the eagle's. Why then should you fair ones be proud of anything that are by other creatures exceeded in all things ?

Amongst the fair women whom Heywood celebrates pre-eminent is the lady of Norwich, whose story, as has been seen, furnished the sub-plot of *The Captives*, and also, considerably transformed, has its place in *The Jew of Malta*.* It may be noted that, for the sake of variety, in this prose version the lady's husband, instead of being a Duke is " a Knight . . . whose name is still upon record, being eminent and of note with Henry the fifth, as personally with him in all the wars in France."

Another story, very tenuously connected with fair women, is interesting because through a change in spelling and pronunciation it has now completely lost its point. A young scholar wooed and won a fair maid, the daughter of a Vicar. Afterwards a patron bestowed upon him a Parsonage. Father and son-in-law meeting in a market town fell into controversy as to which was the better man. " The old man he stood upon his gravity, and the name of father ; the young man pleaded that in regard he was a Parson and the other but a Vicar that he was the better of the two." The young man asserted that in a few words he could prove himself the worthier for name, place, and antiquity (p. 262).

*See pp. 50–2.

" Now young knave," said that old Vicar, " what can'st thou say for thyself?" " I only desire " answered that young man " to be resolved in one question." " Propound it " saith the other. " Marry thus," saith he, " *When the world was destroyed in the general deluge, all save eight Parsons, tell me, where were the Vicars then?*" The old man was blank and the young man carried it.

In Book VI treating of Chaste Women and of Women Wantons Heywood among the former thinks it not out of course " to insert a history memorable for the rareness thereof to all posterity," for which he quotes Suidas as the primary authority (p. 271).

It was a custom among the Jewish nation, at what time the holy Temple was yet standing in Jerusalem, to have continually the number of twenty-two chief and selected Priests (just so many as there be letters in the Hebrew language, or books of the Old Testament), and so often as any one of these was taken away by death, immediately another was elected to succeed in his place, and being chosen (in a book kept in the treasury for that only purpose) expressly to write down his own name, and the names of both his parents, with the days punctually set down of the decease of the one and the succession of the other. Now in the time that Christ was conversant in Judaea, and yet had not showed himself to the world, nor preached the word openly to the people, it happened that one of the Priests of the foresaid number died . . . At length was propounded Jesus the son of the carpenter Joseph (for so they termed him) a man though young, yet for the sanctity of his life, his behaviour, and doctrine above all the rest commended.

As his father Joseph was dead his mother was called to the consistory to give the particulars for registration in the book. Her answer was :

> Certain I am that I brought him into the world, but know no father that he hath from the earth, but by the angel it was told me, that he was the Son of God : *he therefore is the Son of God and me.* This the Priests understanding they called for the Book, which being laid open before them, they caused these words to be inscribed : " Upon such a day deceased such a Priest, born of such and such parents, in whose place by the common and united suffrage of us all is elected JESUS, *the* son of the living GOD and the virgin MARY."

Even in this abbreviated form the story is a striking example of Heywood's narrative power, which is illustrated in different fashion at the beginning of Book VII devoted mainly to love between relatives. But as it bears the name of Polyhymnia, the Muse of Memory, this suggests the introduction of some tales by travellers concerning Russia. One of these gentry (p. 315)

> . . . took occasion to discourse of the cities, the rivers, the manners and dispositions of the people, and, withall, the coldness of the clime, " which in some places " (saith he) " I protest is so extreme that one of my Countrymen and I talking together one morning in the fields, our words, still as we spoke them, froze before us in the air, and that so hard, that such as the next day passed that way might read them as perfectly and distinctly as if they had been text in capital letters," to which one of the gentlemen with great modesty replied " truly, sir, me thinks that should be a dangerous country to speak treason in, especially in the depth of winter."

How convenient it would be for some governments today if there could be such an atmospheric evidence of treason !

Among the medley of classical and medieval reminiscences in this book, of filial, sisterly and conjugal affection Heywood inserts (pp. 333–6) a free translation in couplets of the *Nuptial Cento* of Ausonius, though he does not give his name.

So again in Book VIII treating in its earlier sections of Learned Women and Poetesses he translates from Ovid's *Heroides* the long verse epistle in which Sappho declares her love for Phaon (pp. 389–94). He ends his procession of women notable for learning or poetic gifts by some English examples headed by Queen Elizabeth, mistress of the Greek and Latin tongues, and who in French, Italian and Spanish needed no interpreter, but was able to give answer to such ambassadors in their own language. Others were Lady Jane Grey, " unhappy wife of as unfortunate a husband " ; Lady Arabella Stuart, the author of *Urania* (Lady Mary Wroth), the four daughters of Sir Anthony Cook, and " the beautiful and learned Lady Mary, Countess of Pembroke, the worthy sister to her unmatchable brother, Sir Philip Sidney."

From this noble group he passes in the later sections of Book VIII by what seems to us now a paradoxical transition to Witches. From Circe to Medea he takes his way to more modern instances, but declines to vouch for the truth of stories of witches changing their own shape or transforming others. " My promise is only to acquaint you with such things as I have either read or heard related : which, if they err in anything from truth, blame not me." With this caution he first tells of lycanthropy, men taking the form of wolves, and

then of witches who through a certain cheese turned
the tasters to beasts of burden. One of the stories is of
interest because it might form a postcript to *The Golden
Ass* of Apuleius, translated by Adlington, and also for
the incidental reference to Bankes and his horse (p. 411).
A piper on his road to Rome was by this means changed
by two witches into an ass.

> Who, notwithstanding he had lost his shape, still
> retained his natural reason, and (as one Bankes here
> about this city taught his horse to show tricks by
> which he got much money) so this ass being capable
> of what was taught him, and understanding what he
> was bid to do, showed a thousand several pleasures
> (almost impossible to be apprehended by any un-
> reasonable creature) to all such as came to see him,
> and paid for the sight, in so much that he was sold
> by these witches to a neighbour of theirs for a great
> sum of money.

The buyer was warned by them however not to lead
the ass through water, and the ass hearing this realised
that water might be the means of restoring him to his
human shape. In spite of his master's precautions he
managed to leap into a river and waded out in his own
shape. He then disclosed himself to his late master, and
after examination of all concerned, a disputation there-
on was held in the presence of Pope Leo VII, " before
whom the truth thereof was acknowledged and
recorded."

Another of the witches' misdeeds was to raise storms
at sea, and concerning this Heywood relates what
happened to " a woman of good credit and reputation
whom I have known above these four and twenty years,
and is of the same parish where I now live." While

waiting to take ship at Amsterdam she had lent an old woman some money and received in exchange a kettle as a pledge. When the time of departure came the old woman could not redeem the pledge, which Heywood's neighbour took on shipboard, in spite of the old woman's warning, "Why then carry it away if thou can'st!" Soon a violent storm arose which threatened shipwreck, till suddenly an old woman was seen sitting on the top of the mast, and this was reported to Heywood's neighbour.

" O God," saith she . . . " then the old woman is come after me for her kettle " ; the Master apprehending the business, " Marry and then let her have it," saith he, and takes the kettle, coals and all, and casts them overboard into the sea. But this was no sooner done but the witch dismounts herself from the mast, goes aboard the brass kettle, and in a moment sails out of sight ; the air cleared, the winds grew calm, the tempest ceased, and she had a fair and speedy passage into England : and this the same gentlewoman hath often related.

By the time that he reaches Book IX treating of Women in General Heywood has come to the end of his subject, and is content, in his own words, " to take a brief survey of what hath passed in the eight former books." It will be sufficient therefore to refer to two reflective passages, of which one is the prelude and the other wellnigh the epilogue to this last book. The women of all types of whom Heywood has spoken " are gathered to the earth from whence they came," and " we who are yet breathing do but hourly tread upon our graves." Thus he is led to moralise (p. 420).

These considerations of human frailty (as there is but one life, but many ways to destroy it, but one death, yet a thousand means to hasten it) moves me to persuade all, as well men as women, young or old, noble or base, of both sexes and of what condition soever, to doubly arm themselves with constancy to abide it and courage to entertain it . . . As it is ill to wish death, so it is worse to fear it ; besides as it is base cowardice dishonourably to shun it, so it is mere pusillanimity despairingly to hasten it . . . There is no brawling, but all peace ; no dissension, but all concord, unity and equality.

If Heywood can thus face death with equanimity, it is partly due to his realisation that life has its trials for all, from the highest to the lowest.

One woman I had almost forgotten but better remember her at last than not at all, and strange it is I should do so, since she is still present with the King on his throne, with the General in the camp, the tradesman in his shop, and the ploughman in his cottage ; she is with the scholar in his study, and the statesman in his closet ; she is still at the elbow of every father and mother, and no family can exist without her. In this my work she hath risen early with me in the morning and again sat up with me past midnight ; she will leave no man waking, nor forsake him till she see him fast sleeping. This woman's name is Care.

That the words concerning " this my work " are no exaggeration is confirmed by the Latin note appended at its close, " Opus excogitatum, inchoatun, explicitum, et a typographo excussum, inter septemdecem septimanas. Laus Deo." For a book of this scope to be devised, begun, finished and printed within seventeen weeks was indeed a *tour de force*. And one's wonder grows as one contemplates the list of Heywood's sources compiled by Mr. Robert Grant Martin in Volume XX of *Studies in Philology*. Divided into classical and late Greek, classical and late Latin, medieval and Renaissance Latin, English, French, Italian, they fill twelve pages of the periodical. It is true, of course, as Mr. Martin shows, that Heywood's quotations from Homer and other Greek authors are invariably in Latin, and that he had at most a bowing acquaintance with Greek ; that in drawing upon Latin writers he frequently went astray in his interpretation ; and that his erudition generally was widespread and derivative instead of complying with modern standards of scholarship. But his untiring intellectual curiosity and industry deserve recognition, and he has the credit of being one of the first Englishmen to quote Dante in the original (Parsdiso, XXXIII, 64–6) though not quite accurately.*

> Cosi la neve al sol si disigilla ;
> Cosi al vento nelle foglie lievi,
> Si perdea la sentenza di Sibilla.

While feeling indebted to Mr. Martin for the light that he has thrown upon Heywood's sources in Γυναικεῖον I must dissent from his verdict on his prose style as " a topic which may be dismissed briefly and without enthusiasm." There are, no doubt, long jejune stretches where he was hurriedly dishing up traditional material. But even on the imperfect evidence of the quotations that I have given I would make the claim that Heywood showed remarkable skill in one of the most difficult of literary *genres*, the short story.

---

*Heywood, or the printer has in l. 64 " Come " and " distilla," in l. 65 " leve," and in l. 66 " sententia ".

And in his occasional reflective passages his style attains dignity and an impressively sombre rhythm. If after the fashion of his day, he was too fond of coining ponderous neologisms, he knew both in his poetry and his prose the value of the effect gained by mingling long, resonant and pithy monosyllabic words. His theatrical experience too had taught him the value of contrast on a broader scale. In defending himself for introducing among graver histories lighter jests and tales he pointed to the example of writers for the stage who " lest the auditory should be dulled with serious courses . . . in every Act present some zany with his mimic action to breed in the less capable mirth and laughter, for they that write to all must strive to please all."

In any case it sufficiently pleased E.P. (Edward Phillips, Milton's nephew) for him to revise the book in 1657 as *The General History of Women, Containing the Lives of the most Holy and Prophane, the most Famous and Infamous in all ages*, with the omission of the address to the reader, for which he substituted a new one, and of the dedication.

It might have been thought that with the 466 folio pages of Γυναικεῖον Heywood had exhausted what he had to say on its subject, but he returned to it again in part in 1640 with *The Exemplary Lives and Memorable Acts of Nine the Most Worthy Women of the World*. In his epistle to the General Reader he seeks to justify his action as follows :

It is a kind of duty in all that have had mothers, as far as they can, to dignify the sex, which in my Γυναικεῖον or *History of Women*, I have strived to do with my utmost Minerva ; but that was a

mere miscellany of all ages, sexes, qualities, com-
plexions, conditions, dispositions, of rich, poor,
learned, unlearned, fair, foul, well featured, de-
formed, barren, bearing, matron, meretrix, and all
in general, from the sceptre to the sheephook, from
the Court to the cottage. But in this tractate I have
only commemorated the lives and memorable acts
of nine (alluding to the number of the Muses), three
Jews, three Gentiles, three Christians.

This epistle is part of the elaborate prefatory material. It has two dedicatory addresses, one in prose
to " the excellently disposed Mistress Elizabeth, the
Virtuous Consort of Clovill Tanfield of Copt-Fold
Hall in Essex, Esquire " : the other in verse " to the
honourable and eminently virtuous, the excellent Lady
Theophila, the learned Consort of the right worthy
Sir Robert Cook, Knight &c. " These are followed by
an epistle " to all noble and brave-spirited gentlemen,
with the excellent and virtuously disposed gentle-
women in general," after which comes the already mentioned epistle to the general reader. Then succeed
four verse tributes in praise of the work by William Ball,
Stephen Bradwell, Thomas Brewer and George Estont-
wile to Heywood, variously described as " much re-
spected friend " " learned, loving friend," etc.
    The three Jewish female worthies are Deborah,
Judith, and Esther ; the three Gentiles are Bonduca or
Boadicea, Penthesilea, queen of the Amazons, and
Artemisia, the Carian queen ; the three Christians are
Elflida, wife of Ethelred, duke of Mercia, Margaret,
queen of Henry VI, and Elizabeth of England. Of each
of these a portrait is given in martial or regal array,
Judith holding the severed head of Holofermes. The
attractive contrasting frontispiece of an unnamed lady

in what might be court dress, I feel tempted to con-
jecture is one of the two dedicatees.

But *The Exemplary Lives* cannot be said to be worthy
of all this prefatory and illustrative paraphernalia. The
accounts of them, in each case preluded by a page of
rhymed couplets facing the portrait, are in the case of
the first seven " women worthies " merely versions of
Biblical or legendary sources. With Queen Margaret,
married almost exactly two centuries before the publication of *Exemplary Lives*, Heywood comes closer to
authentic history. And his presentation of her has the
interest of comparing her favourably with Shakespeare's unflattering picture of her in *King Henry VI*,
Parts II and III. Her dauntless courage outweighed, in
Heywood's eyes, all her failings. As he sums up her
character in the closing lines of his verse tribute to her :

Who can this Queen's heroic spirit express ?
A foe to peace ; in field a championess.
Usurping all that Majesty could claim,
Leaving her husband nothing save his name.
He wears the Crown ; she sword and sceptre bore.
What could the brave Semiramis do more ?

Concerning Elizabeth he could add nothing new to
his oft repeated praise. But the portrait of her with
crown and sceptre, and in regally elaborate costume
is not of the most striking presentation of his adored
queen.

CHAPTER 9

The Hierarchy of The Blessed Angels

In 1635, thirty-six years after the publication of *Troia Britannica*, there came from Heywood's pen another full-length poem, *The Hierarchy of the Blessed Angels : Their Names, Orders, and Offices. The Fall of Lucifer with his Angels.* Printed, like Γυναικεῖον, by Adam Islip it was a folio volume of 630 pages in nine Books. As each of the nine Books of Γυναικεῖον had been called after one of the Muses so each of the nine Books of *The Hierarchy* was named after an angel or archangel. Fronting the engraved title-page is the licence for printing of William Heywood, domestic chaplain of the Archbishop of Canterbury. Each Book is preceded by an engraving, paid for by a different sponsor, a remarkable personal tribute to Heywood. Three of these engravings are reproduced in the present volume.

Even in that age of flowery and flattering dedications that of *The Hierarchy* is outstanding.

To the most excellent and incomparable Lady, as famous for her illustrious virtues, as fortunate in her regal issue ; Henrietta Maria, Queen : The Royal Consort and Spouse of the Puissant and Invincible Monarch, our dread Sovereign, King Charles : Her Highness most lowly and loyal subject, Thomas Heywood, in all humility consecrateth these his well-wishing, though unworthy, Labours.

[123]

I wonder how much Henrietta Maria read of these
" well-wishing labours." But Heywood seems at this
time to have been in desperate need of beneficial
patronage, to judge from such a complaint as this.

A sycophant or ballading Knave,
If he but impudence and gay clothes have
Can harp upon some scurrilous jest or tale,
(though fifteen times told and in 'th'city stale)
Command a great man's ear ; perhaps be able
To prefer suits and elbow at his table,
Wear speaking pockets ; boast whom he doth serve
When meriting men may either beg or starve.

The Hierarchy begins with an argument for the existence of God.

That there's a God who doubts ? who dares dispute,
Being in itself a maxim absolute ?
Which fundamental truth, as it is seen
In all things, light or dark, wither'd or green :
In length, breadth, height, depth, what is done or
    said,
Or hath existence in this fabric, made
By the word *Fiat* : so amongst the rest
In man's own conscience it is deep'st exprest.

And from this the poem takes its meandering way
through sacred and secular history, quoting from the
Bible, the Fathers of the Church, classical historians
and poets, *et hoe genus omne.* Even allowing for the fact
that Heywood doubtless drew, after the fashion of his
age, upon compendia and cyclopaedios the erudition
and industry displayed are astonishing. He first proceeds to trace the origin of Idolatry and Superstition,
" Yet these did worship something " (p. 11). It has
been left to his own day to produce the atheist.

> This Age breeds men so brutish natural
> As to believe there is no God at all.

In lofty verse Heywood bids them look upward and
downward and find God both ways.

> Would such but spend a little vacant time
> To look from what's below to things sublime :
> From terrene to celestial and confer
> The universal with what's singular,
> They shall find nothing so immense and high
> Beyond their stubborn, dull capacity,
> But figures unto them His magnitude.
> Again nothing so slight, as to exclude
> It(s) name among His creatures, nought so small,
> But proves to them its power majestical.

Amongst the various types of atheists Heywood has
special scorn for those who merely make a pretence of
piety for worldly advantage (p. 19).

> Divers will seem religious to comply
> With time and place, but ask their reason why
> They so conform themselves, they know no cause.
> More than to save their purse and keep the laws,
> There be to noble houses make resort,
> And sometimes elbow great men at the Court,
> Who, though they seem to bear things fair and well,
> Yet would turn Moses into Machiavel.

And with such hypocrisy he links, incongruously as it
now seems, scepticism about the accuracy of the Old
Testament, when they

> Reckon up genealogies who were
> Long before Adam, and without all fear,
> As those doom'd to the bottomless Abysm,
> Hold there was no Noah's ark nor Cataclysm.

This inevitably recalls the accusations against Raleigh's and Harriot's School of Atheism, and in particular the statement attributed by Richard Baines to Marlowe that " the Indians and many authors of antiquity have assuredly written of above 16 thousande yeares agone, whereas Adam is proved to have lived within 6 thowsand yeares."

From the atheist who denies that there is a God Heywood turns in Book II to confute those who believe in more Gods than one (p. 67).

> If God be perfect, he can be but one
> As having all things in himself alone.
> The more you make, the more you shall deprave
> Their might and potency, as those that have
> Their virtue scanted ; so allow not any,
> Since all things cannot be contain'd in *Many* ;
> By which 'tis manifest, those that maintain
> More gods than one be people vile and vain,
> In the like blasphemy ready to fall
> With the damn'd atheist, who knows none at all.

In Book III Heywood passes from the Workman, God, to his work, the universe, which he represents as in three divisions the super-celestial the abode of angels, the celestial or ethereal, containing the stars, and the elementary, the dwelling of man, beast and all mortal creatures. He expands this with a wealth of illustrations, scriptural, philosophic, classical and anecdotal, ending with caustic ridicule of Plato's concept of a great recurring year (p. 148).

>   If this were true,
> The books which we write now before were new ;
> And by all such as now peruse them read ;
> And in the future, having long been dead,

When this year *vertent* comes, we shall again
Be born as heretofore ; on earth remain
In the same time and lead the self-same lives,
Have the same neighbours, marry the same wives.

In Book IV he raises his eyes from earth (p. 193-4).

Unto the glorious Hierarchy above,
The blest degrees in which the Angels move
  * * * * *
Immortal, incorporeal, moving still,
Assisting man, obedient to God's will,
In three most blessed Hierarchies th'are guided
And each into three companies divided.

Heywood describes these different orders, with their
special functions, and then turns to confute those
" pretending no small judgement " who deny the
existence of angels and of spirits altogether. He cites
against such sceptics the views of Plato, Plotinus and
other Greek Philosophers. He appeals to the evidence
of dreams and visions recorded in the Scriptures and
by classical writers. He then passes somewhat irrelevantly to the unique power of poetry to defeat all-con-
quering Death, whose victims are detailed in sombrely
impressive lines (p. 204).

What's gentry then ? or noblesse ? greatness, what ?
The civil purple ? or the clergy hat ?
The coronet or mitre ? nay the crown
Imperial ? what's potency ? renown ?
Ovations, triumphs, with victorious bays ?
Wisdom or wealth ? Can these add to thy days ?
Inquire of Roman Brutus, surnamed Just,
Or Solomon the Wise, they both are dust,

Learn'd Aristotle, Plato the Divine,
From earth they came, and, earth, they now are thine,
Where are the worthies, where the rich or fair ?
All in one common bed involved are.

*   *   *   *   *

Consider well the misery of man
And weigh it truly, since there's none but can
Take from his own and others, thousand ways,
But yet not add one minute to their days.

Should not then the poet, who alone can bestow life
after death, be held in high honour ?

How in these days is such a man regarded ?
No, not so much as oil or ink rewarded.

unless he is one of the sycophantic tribe described
above. It was different in antiquity, and here Heywood
uses a curiously unconvincing argument, though it has
an undesigned fortunate result for us. Poets of old were
honoured by the " swelling styles," by which they were
known, the most of them graced with three names at
least, e.g., Publius Virgilius Maro, Publius Terentius
Afer, but now,

Our modern Poets to that pass are driven
Those names are curtail'd which they first had given
And, as we wished to have their memories drown'd,
We scarcely can afford them half their sound.

There follows a passage for which alone, remote as it is
from the subject of angels, it was worth while writing this
ponderous tome, and which brings us closer into the
company of the Elizabethan wits in undress, so to
speak, than any other known to me (p. 206).

Engraving prefixed to "The Virtues," Book V of *The
Hierarchy of the Blessed Angels*, with the Crucifixion in the
foreground.

Thom: Hammon Armig: Rich: Gethinge M^r of y^e pen.

Engraving prefixed to " The Angel," Book IX of *The Hierarchy of the Blessed Angels*, with the Blessed on the right hand and the Damned on the left.

Greene who had in both Academies ta'ne
Degree of Master, yet could never gain
To be call'd more than Robin ; who, had he
Profest ought save the Muse, serv'd and been free
After a seven years prenticeship might have
(With credit too) gone Robert to his grave.
Marlo, renown'd for his rare art and wit,
Could ne'er attain beyond the name of Kit,
Although his *Hero and Leander* did
Merit addition rather. Famous Kid
Was call'd but Tom ; Tom Watson, though he wrote
Able to make Apollo's self to dote
Upon his Muse, for all that he could strive.
Yet never could to his full name arrive,
Tom Nash (in his time of no small esteem)
Could not a second syllable redeem.
Excellent Beaumont, in the foremost rank
Of the rar'st wits, was never more than Frank,
Melliflous Shakespeare, whose enchanting quill
Commanded mirth or passion, was but Will.
And famous Johnson, though his learned pen
Be dipt in Castaly, is still but Ben,
Fletcher and Webster, of that learned pack
None of the mean'st, yet neither was but Jack.
Dekker but Tom, nor May, nor Middleton,
And he's now but Jack Ford, that once were John.

Then not quite consistently with the contrast that
he has drawn between classical and modern usage,
Heywood goes on to declare :

                I, for my part,
(Think others what they please) accept that heart
Which courts my love in most familiar phrase,
And that it takes not from my pains or praise
If any one to me so bluntly come ;
I hold he loves me best that calls me Tom.

Among those who loved Heywood were not those playwrights of a younger generation whom he denounces
for their malicious jealousy (p. 208).

How comes it, ere he know it
A puny shall assume the name of poet,
And in a tympa'nous* and thrasonic style
(Words at which th'ignorant laugh but the learn'd
    smile
Because adulterate and undenizen'd) he
Should task such artists as have took degree
Before he was a freshman, and because,
No good practitioner in the stage's laws,
He miss'd th'applause he aim'd at, he'll devise
Another course his fame t'immortalise,
Imploring divers pens, failing his own,
To support that which others have cried down.

In Book V Heywood discourses further of the relation
between the various orders of the hierarchy of angels
and the celestial universe, from the *Primum Mobile* to
the sphere of the moon. He then passes to a comparison
of the three chief religions. He thus interprets the plea
of the Jews (p. 284).

What people can there be
That dares in noblesse or antiquity
With our blest Hebrew nation to contend ?
For who's so dull that knows not we descend
From Prophets, Kings and Patriarchs, who pretend
That this one offspring lineally came
From our great predecessor, Abraham

As to the Mahometan :

He cavils with the Christian, and thus says,
None like to us the great Creator praise ;
We only unto One make adoration,
Whereas the Christian sect build their salvation

*Inflated.

Upon a son (this God should have) and He
Equal to Him from all eternity ;
Proceeding further, should there be two gods,
They of necessity should fall at odds,
Since supreme Powers equality abhor,
And are impatient of competitor.

Having thus stated the case for these two religions, Heywood merely opposes to the vain tradition of the Hebrews the infallible testimony of the sacred Scriptures. He then with evident gusto proceeds to expose the " delirements of the devilish Alcoran " from which he quotes at length a number of its " blasphemous fictions." This detailed indictment throws a fierce light on the animosity of seventeenth century Englishmen to " Mahound " and his followers.

Book VI opens with a meditation on the waywardness of the human heart which can only first rest (as Heywood almost seems to echo the words of St. Augustine) in submission to the only true and living God (p. 333).

To whom we cannot come, tow'rds whom not move
But by the steps of charity and love :
In whom no int'rest we can have, unless
In all things we humility profess :
Nor can we humble be, so to aspire,
Unless by industry the truth t'acquire.

After this poem Heywood reverts to the problems connected with the creation of angels, followed by that of man, and to the revelation by God to the Angels that his Son would take on him human nature. It was this that inspired the rebellion of Lucifer and the war in Heaven between his followers and those of the Archangel Michael. Heywood's conception of this great "angelonachy" is less material than that of Milton some thirty years later (p. 341).

> No lances, swords, nor bombards they had then,
> Or other weapons now in use with men ;
> None of the least material substance made ;
> Spirits by such give no offence or aid.
> Only spiritual arms to them were lent,
> And these were call'd affectionate Consent,
> Now both of these in Lucifer, the Devil,
> And his complies immoderate were and evil,
> Those that in Michael, the Archangel, reign'd
> And his good spirits meekly were maintain'd,
> Squar'd and directed by th'Almighty's will
> (The rule by which they fight and conquer still)

This leads up to a discussion of the nature of Hell, to which Lucifer and his crew fall. Classical poets and Biblical writers are in turn called in witness and finally Heywood turns with verse Lucian's dialogue, *Necyamantia* to show "how he and suchlike Atheists jest at Hell."

Book VII returns to the fallen angels who after being "extruded" from the hierarchies (p. 411)

> Have amongst them orders and degrees,
> And though the benefit of grace they leese,
> Yet still that natural power and force retain,
> At first bequeath'd them, being reduc'd again
> To order, and their offices still keep,
> As once in heaven, so in th'infernal deep.

Lucifer is the "prime Captain and King," and to describe him Heywood once again borrows not quite accurately from Dante,* quoting in the original Italian

*See page 119.

(Inferno XXXIV, 28 ff.) the twenty-seven lines beginning :

L'Imperador del Doloroso Regno,

of which he also gives a free moralising interpretation.
Under him the evil angels are ranged in degrees of
priority (p. 414).

> Nor do the lower of bad Spirits obey
> Those of superior office because they
> Or love them or esteem them. The cause why
> They yield themselves to such priority
> Is for that th'other have more power, and can
> With greater subtlety insidiate man.

Heywood then goes off at a tangent for more than
900 lines, relating an " excellent history " of a Greek
family, where the Devil with his " anti-mask " sought
in vain to frustrate the intentions of God. The story is
in itself interesting and is well told, but in its dispro-
portionate length it is out of place. From it Heywood
returns to the nine orders of the rebellious fallen angels
with their respective leaders, and then passes to an
inquisition into the motion of angels, good or evil
(p. 438).

>   Know then, he
> Is not contain'd in place, as brutes and we,
> But place itself he in himself contains,
> Being said to be still when his power remains,
> And though it pass our weak ingeniousity
> Yet he is known to be of strange velocity,
> And without passing places can with ease
> Or go or come at all times when he please.
> From heaven to earth he can descend and be
> Above and here in space unmomentary ;
> Hence, thence he (undisturb'd) hath passage fair
> Through both the elements of fire and air.

Another distinguishing mark of angels is the certainty, within limits, of their knowledge (p. 442).

> Spirits cannot err and be deceiv'd as we,
> Seeing and knowing all things perfectly
> In their true real essence, which is meant
> Only of natural things, and hath extent
> No further. For, as angels creatures be
> Th'are limited in their capacity :
> In all such things as on God's power depend
> Or man's free-will, their skill is at an end,
> And understand no further than reveal'd
> By the Creator ; else 'tis shut and seal'd.

In Book VIII Heywood recounts the various temptations with which evil spirits beset human beings. Among them are the *Incubi* who have intercourse with women and the *Succubi* in like fashion with men. There are also spirits of fire, air and water. In illustration of the malign workings of all these pestilent beings Heywood relates tales. And what is of special interest, and seems to have gone unnoticed, is that as Shakespeare, in compliment to King James, had dramatised the story of Macbeth and Banquo, so Heywood some twenty years later, citing not Shakespeare but Boece as his authority, tells in semi-dialogue form the same story in honour of King Charles. The two Scottish nobles encounter in a dark grove " three virgins wondrous fair " (p. 508).

> The first of them did curtsey low, her veil
> Unpinn'd, and with obedience said, " All hail !
> Mackbeth, Thane Glamus." The next said,
> " All hail ! Caldarius Thane," the third said,
> " Not the least honour unto thee I bring,
> Mackbeth, all hail ! that shortly must be King."

These spake no more ; when Banco thus replied,
" I'll have ye done, fair ladies, to divide
Me from all honours : how comes he thus grown
In your great grace, to promise him a crown?
And I, his sole companion, as you see,
Yet you in nothing deign to guerdon me."
To whom the first made answer, " Yet, we bring
To thee much happier fate for though a King
Mackbeth shall be, yet shall he reign alone,
And leave no issue to succeed his throne,
And thou, O Banco, though thou dost not sway
Thyself a sceptre, yet thine issue may,
And so it shall : thine issue (do not fear)
Shall govern Scotland many a happy year."
This spoke, all vanished.

The pair were first amazed at the " strange novel "*
and thinking that they had seen " vain spectres "
speaking mere fiction, they saluted each other in jest
as " King " and " Grandsire of Kings." How different from Shakespeare's presentation, and how un-
suitable the tale as an example of demoniac jugglery
for the predictions proved true.

In process the crown lineally descended
To Banco's issue, and is yet extended
In ample genealogy, remaining
In most renowned CHARLES, amongst us reigning.

Another tale from Scottish annals illustrates the
malign influence of Spectres of whom the sight betokens
imminent death. King Alexander III being without
issue made a third marriage (p. 511).

In the mid revels the first ominous night
Of their espousals, when the moon shone bright,

*News.

With lighted tapers, the King and the Queen leading
The curious* measures, lords and ladies treading
The self-same strains ; the King looks back by chance
And spies a strange intruder fill the dance,
Namely a mere Anatomy, quite bare,
His naked limbs both without flesh and hair,
(As we decipher Death) who stalks about,
Keeping the measure till the dance was out,
The King with all the rest affrighted stand ;
The Spectre vanished and then strict command
Was giv'n to break up revels, each 'gan fear
This omen, and presage disaster near.

And so it befell. The King soon after fell from his
horse and died, and there followed " sedition, wreck
and ruin."

At the beginning of the ninth and last Book Heywood
suddenly versifies from Esdras in the Apocrypha a discussion between three young men at the Court of King
Darius as to " what thing should strongest be." The
first speaker makes the claim for Wine (p. 564).

For needs must that be said to tyrannise
Which tames the strong, and doth deceive the wise.
The mind it alters, and 'tis that alone
That makes the sceptre and the sheep-hook one :
For you in wine no difference can see
Betwixt the poor and rich, the bond and free.
It glads the heart and makes the thoughts forget
Trouble and sorrow, servitude and debt

The second speaker maintains that the King is strongest
for he has all men at his command (p. 565).

If he bid smile, they smile, or, if he frown,
And bid demolish, all things are torn down.

*Intricate.

If he say build, they build, or, if destroy,
All goes to havoc : and yet he in joy
Meantime sits down, doth eat, doth drink, doth sleep,
And all the rest a watch about him keep.
Neither can any tend his own affairs,
But the King's only ; every man prepares
To do him service (reason too) for they
Dare not but his great potency obey.

The third speaker claims that Woman is more powerful
than Wine or King. Man is born from her and cannot
live without her (p. 565).

If he hath gath'red silver, or got gold,
Or found out aught that's precious to behold,
Doth he not bring it to his choice Delight,
Her that is fair and precious in his sight ?
Leaves he not all his business and affair
To gaze upon her eyes, play with her hair ?

   *   *   *   *   *

Man leaves his father, mother, country, all
(What he esteems most dear) to become thrall
In voluntary bondage with his wife,
To lead a private and contented life,
Which life for her he hazardeth, and her
'Fore father, mother, country doth prefer.

Then by an unheralded and abrupt transition he proceeds to assert that Truth is the strongest of all things :
(p. 567)

She's the strength, kingdom, power, dignity,
And of all ages sovereign majesty.
Blest be the GOD of Truth ! At this he stay'd.
Then all the people cry'd aloud and said
With public suffrage " Truth is great'st and strongest,
Which (as it was at first) shall endure longest."

This might have formed a fitting climax to the *Hierarchy*, but the ninth Book had to be filled and Heywood turns his attention to Subterranean Spirits or Mountain Dwarfs who play havoc with the work of miners, cause earthquakes, and fake precious metals. And if Heywood had seen on the stage or read Marlowe's *Doctor Faustus*, it is disconcerting that his only allusion to the Doctor is to a piece of knavish trickery (p. 574).

> Of Faustus and Agrippa it is told
> That in their travels they bare seeming gold,
> Which would abide the touch ; and by the way
> In all their hostries they would freely pay.
> But parted thence, mine host, thinking to find
> Those glorious pieces they had left behind
> Safe in his bag, sees nothing save together
> Round scuts of horn and pieces of old leather.

Yet another order of spirits are those that detest the light of day, and are called Pugs, or Hobgoblins or Robin goodfellows (p. 574).

> In solitary rooms these uproars keep,
> And beat at doors to wake men from their sleep,
> Seeming to force locks, be they ne'er so strong,
> And keeping Christmas gambols all night long.
> Pots, glasses, trenchers, dishes, pans and kettles
> They will make dance about the shelves and settles,
> As if about the kitchen tost and cast,
> Yet in the morning nothing found misplac't.

Finally Heywood raises the question of how we are to distinguish between good and bad spirits, for both can forsake their shapes and figures and take bodily form. But there are revealing differences. Good angels " still take the shape of man " ; evil spirits, if they do

so, have some " strange prodigious mark," like a goat's
foot or a satyr's forehead. But usually they (p. 480)

> In figures more contemptible appear,
> One like a wolf, another like a bear :
> Others resembling dogs, apes, monkeys, cats,
> And sometimes birds as crows, pies, owls, and bats.
> But never hath it yet been read or told
> That ever cursed spirit should be so bold
> To show his damned head amongst them all
> In th'innocent lambs or doves that have no gall.

Then again, and this time with an apology, Heywood
goes off at a tangent to celebrate the music of the
spheres and of the heavenly hosts (p. 582).

> Something I had forgot in my great speed.
> Of Music then, e're further I proceed,
> I must derive it from the first of days.
> The spheres chime music to their Maker's praise,
> In the world's first creation it begun
> From the word *Fiat* spoke and it was done ;
> Was sound and sweetness, voice, and symphony,
> Concord, concent, and heavenly harmony.
> The three great orders of the Hierarchy,
> Servants unto th'eternal Majesty,
> In their degrees of termines* hourly sing
> Loud Hallelujahs to th'almighty King ;
> The Seraphins, the Cherubims and Thrones,
> Potestates, Virtues, Dominations,
> The Principates, Archangels, Angels, all
> Resound his praise in accents musical.

Thus in this roundabout way Heywood reverts to his
original theme of the Hierarchy of the Blessed Angels.
But the music of the spheres leads him on to the motions

*Limits.

of the planets, and it is noticeable that his account of some of their revolutions, tallies, as far as it goes, practically with that which Marlowe puts into the mouth of Faustus.

> As first, in nine and twenty days the Moon,
> The Sun and Venus in one twelvemonth theirs,
> And Saturn his in thirty complete years.

But unlike Marlowe Heywood, in spite of his multifarious learning, has little sympathy with the toilers after " knowledge infinite," whose ambition is " Mysteries to search, and dive in arts profound." He makes mock of the different sects and schools of philosophy, at variance with one another (p. 586).

> Then to conclude, studies that have foundation,
> Like these, upon man's mere imagination
> Than the chameleons are more variable,
> Lighter than wind, than the sea more unstable ;
> Than th'elements th'are at more deadly bate
> And than the labyrinth more intricate,
> Than th'moon more changing, darkness more obscure,
> Than women more inconstant and unsure.

There is only one infallible source and best of knowledge, the Bible (p. 587).

>   Now, if any
> Of the great Doctors differ (as th'are many),
> Retire we to the Scriptures, the true test,
> To know of their opinions which sounds best,
> Nor let their works further authoris'd be
> Than punctually they with the Text agree :
> Neither let any, of his knowledge proud,
> Dare further search than is by them allow'd.

Hence it is in the same spirit of humility as St. Augustine that Heywood takes his leave.

> Whoso shall read this work, where he shall find
> Truth certain, let him join with me in mind :
> When he shall doubt with me I next desire
> That he with me will labour to inquire :
> If he have err'd in judgment and find here
> To be resolv'd, from hence his error clear.
> If he my error find (with some respect
> Of my good meaning) let him mine correct.

A tribute to *The Hierarchy* was paid in 1640, the year before Heywood's death, by an anonymous critic in *Wit's Recreation*, who evidently liked Heywood much better as poet and writer of prose than as dramatist.

> Thou hast writ much and art admir'd by those
> Who love the easy rambling of thy prose ;
> But yet thy pleasing'st flight was somewhat high
> When thou did'st touch the angels' hierarchy.
> Fly that way still ; it will become thy age,
> And better please than grovelling on the stage.

On the other hand Cowley in 1656 delivered a blow which might have made Heywood turn in his grave :

" If any man design to compose a sacred poem by only turning a story of Scripture, like Mr. Quarles, or some other godly matter like Mr. Heywood of angels, into rhyme, he is so far from elevating poetry that he only abuses divinity."

No fair-minded critic can endorse this unqualified stricture. It is true that Heywood too often let his pen meander at will, and that, in spite of its division into nine Books, *The Hierarchy* as a whole, is a somewhat formless product. He also clogged each of the Books by appending to it a series of theological, philosophical, historical, emblematical and other Observations, mainly in prose, and a Meditation in verse. Nor today can we give the ready acceptance that is needed for the appreciation of Heywood's unquestioning belief in and presentation of the different orders of angels and evil spirits. Nor can we acquiesce in the " fundamentalist " attitude that refers every question to the infallible verdict of a Biblical text.

None the less *The Hierarchy*, apart from its interesting incidental contemporary allusions, is a work of higher quality and value than appears at first sight. It deals with some of the loftiest themes that a poet can choose. In seeking to analyse and illustrate many of the ultimate problems concerning God and man Heywood can range from almost metaphysical subtlety to a well-nigh majestic ring, and thence again to colloquial ease of tone. It was his ill fortune that in so much of its mighty theme *The Hierarchy* some thirty years later was to be overshadowed by Milton's architectonic genius in *Paradise Lost*.

CHAPTER 10

*Pleasant Dialogues and Dramas—London Mayoral
Pageants—Last Plays*

In *The Hierarchy of the Blessed Angels* Heywood had
for once soared into " an ampler ether, a diviner air,"
but the fascination of classical legend and mythology
was inexhaustible for him, and in his collection of
Pleasant Dialogues and Dramas published in 1637, the
predominant part is played by his versification of
fifteen of Lucian's *Dialogues*. Were it nothing more, this
teaching of Greek prose (perhaps through some intermediary version) " to go upon even feet and number,"
in English (as Heywood puts it) would be a notable
tour de force. But I cannot agree with Dr. Clark in dis-
missing these renderings of Lucian (together with the
rest of the volume) as " awkward, uninspired and dull."
Judged by Elizabethan standards they are adequately
close to the originals. And, in my opinion, they show
Heywood's mastery of the rhymed couplet, both closed
and run-on. Some examples may be taken from the first
and longest of his Lucian translations, *The Man-haters*.
Timon is expatiating to Jupiter, now that he is in deep
poverty, on the baseness of those who paid him court in
his days of wealth.

If (as sometimes) I chance to cross the street,
And any one of these my creatures meet,
As of some statue, by long time decayed,
They shun my shadow, of my fall afraid :

And others likewise that from far espy me
Into some by-lane screw themselves, to fly me,
Make me an ominous spectacle of Fate,
As if malevolent and unfortunate ;
Who in my better days was their director,
Styled by themselves their father and protector.
These mischiefs growing, to be made so vile,
My own deep counsels I 'gan reconcile,
Snatcht up this mattock, choos'd a field out where
The earth's fair breast I am forced to wound and
    bear,
And thus my time in labour wear away,
Being hired for some four half pence by the day.

Or take Jupiter's cynical description to Mercury of
men's confused philosophic wranglings :

I cast mine eye of late on Athens, where
So many strange duels and fencings were,
Such *Pro's* and *Contra's*, quarrels in the schools,
Like mad men railing, some ; others, like fools
Gibing ; in uproar all, shrill acclamations
Of scolding disputants ; such vociferations.

       *   *   *   *   *

There's a new toy imagined by those Noddies
Of things essential and yet wanting bodies,
Mere fantasies, which they with might and main
(Though nothing) to have being would maintain.

When Jove sends Plutos, the god of wealth, to restore
Timon to his former prosperity he at first indignantly
refuses his gifts.

Excellent Poverty contrariwise
Inur'd me unto pains and exercise
Becoming Man ; truly and freely we
Together liv'd in consociety,

Supplying me with all things, garments, meat,
Which tasted best being season'd with my sweat,
All vulgar things she taught me to despise,
And look on frailties with unpartial eyes,
Persuading me that Hope hath steadfast root
Where man's own industry's assistant to't.

Even when he turns up golden treasure with his spade
and becomes enriched again he determines to lead a
sad and solitary life " for only Timon shall be Timon's
friend," and he rebuffs with blows and insults the false
friends and flatterers who seek him out again.

Illustrating Heywood's command of cut and thrust
repartee is his version of the dialogue between Charon,
Menippus and Mercury.

Char. Pay me my fare, thou witch.
Men.   Nay, scold outright,
If thou to hear thyself speak tak'st delight.
Char. My due for thy trajection down here lay.
Men. I prithee, how can he that hath not, pay ?
Char. Is't possible there any one can be
That is not worth a single halfpenny ?
Men. I know not to whom else thou pratest here,
But for mine own part I have none, I swear.
Char. I'll baste thee with this ship-rope, if my hire
Thou tend'rest not.
Men.   Then shall my staff aspire
To fly about thine ears.
Char.   So long a cut
Must I take pains to waft thee, and thou put
To no expense at all ?
Men.   Let Hermes stand
Engag'd for me, who gave me to thine hand.
Merc. By Jove in time I shall be ill bestead,
If I be put to pay fares for the dead.

Menippus asserts that he has worked his passage by
first pumping and then tugging at the oar, and when
Charon answers that these are nothing to his fare, he
asks to be borne back to life. This is not possible, as
indeed Menippus knows, for when Charon warns,
" Well, if again I take him here," he retorts,

> Thou threatenest me in vain.
> This passage, though not far 'twixt shore and shore,
> Yet once being passed, cannot be travelled more.

Menippus appears again in another *Dialogue* of Lucian
of which Heywood includes a translation not in this
volume but among the Observations appended to
Book IV of *The Hierarchy of the Blessed Angels*. There he is
not quarrelling with Charon about the fare, but setting
an example for other Ghosts by stripping himself naked
as they all must do, if the boat is not to be overweighted
by their earthly possessions.

That Lucian made a special appeal to Heywood is
clear from the tribute that he went out of his way to
pay to him in his discussion of atheism in Book I of
The Hierarchy (pp. 14–15).

> Unhappy Lucian, what sad passionate verse
> Shall I bestow upon the marble stone
> That covers thee ? How shall I deck thy herse,
> With bays or cypress ? I do not bemoan
> Thy death, but that thou died'st thus. Had thy creed
> As firm been as thy wit fluent and high,
> All that have read thy works would have agreed
> To have transferr'd thy soul above the sky,
> And sainted thee. But, oh 'tis to be doubted
> The God thou didst despise will thee expel
> From his blest place, and since thou Heav'n hast
>   flouted,
> Confine thy soul into thine own made Hell.

The versified dialogues from Erasmus and Textor, and the " emblems of rich conceit " from Catsius, are little more than literary curiosities.   But the two short dramas, suggested by the *Metamorphoses, Jupiter and Io* and *Apollo and Daphne* would not have been unfit for inclusion in the *Ages*. The Prologues and Epilogues, chiefly spoken before royalty on theatrical or domestic occasions, or before the Earl of Dover on festival nights, have special interest for dramatic historians.

Heywood's classical interests were even to influence his work in a very different field. His pride in London and its famous citizens has been illustrated from several of his plays. It was therefore a fitting compliment that he should have been invited by the Haberdashers' Company in 1631 to provide the pageant for the inauguration of one of the Company as Lord Mayor. As this London office corresponded to that of the Roman Praetor whose authority was styled *Jus Honorarium* Heywood gave the title of *London's Jus Honorarium* to his piece. It began with a show on the water, where Ulysses who " personated a wise and discreet magistrate," steered his way between Scylla and Charybdis with the cautionary cry :

Keep the even channel and be neither swayed
To the right hand nor left, and so evade
Malicious envy, never out of action,
Smooth-visaged flattery and black-mouthed de-
    traction ;
Sedition, whisperings, murmuring, private hate,
All ambushing the godlike Magistrate.

Of the shows that follow on land the most striking " presented in the upper part of Cheapside " was the second. London is represented by a lady seated in a chariot with Justice and Mercy riding before her, the one on a lion, the other on a unicorn. Beside and behind her are ladies representing various chief cities of the Kingdom, Westminster, York, Bristol, Oxford, Lincoln, etc., whom she welcomes.

> You noble cities of this generous isle
> May these my two each ladies ever smile,
> Justice and Mercy, on you ! You, we know,
> Are come to grace this our triumphant show,
> And, of your courtesy, the hand to kiss
> Of London, this fair land's Metropolis,
>
>   *   *   *   *   *
>
> Will you know whence proceeds this fair increase,
> This joy, the fruits of a continued peace,
> The way to thrive ; to prosper in each calling,
> The weak and shrinking states to keep from falling ;
> Behold ! my motto shall all this display ;
> Read and observe it well, *serve and obey.*

It is the motto of the Haberdashers' Company which Heywood applies to the City as a whole, and whose significance he thus interprets :

> *Obedience,* though it humbly doth begin,
> It soon augments unto a magazin
> Of plenty ; in all cities 'tis the ground,
> And doth like harmony in music sound.
> Nations and commonweals by it alone
> Flourish : it incorporates many into one,
> And makes unanimous peace, content and joy,
> Which pride doth still insidiate to destroy.

Besides thus expounding the motto of the Haberdashers Heywood in the third show " near unto the Great Cross in Cheapside," introduces St. Catherine, patron saint of the Company, seated in front of a palace on the top of which is a " glorious presence which personates Honour," who thus addresses the Lord Mayor :

> The way to me, though not debarred,
> Yet it is difficult and hard,
>
>   *   *   *   *   *
>
> So you, and such as you, grave Lord,
> Who wear this Scarlet, use that Sword,
> Collar, and Cap of Maintenance :
> These are no things that come by chance,
> Or got by sleeping, but averse
> From these I am gain'd : by care, commerce,
> The hazarding of goods and men
> To pirates, rocks, shelves,* tempest, when ?†
> You through a wilderness of seas
> Dangers of wreck, surprise, disease,
> Make new discoveries, for a lasting story
> Of this our Kingdom's fame and nation's glory.

Heywood concludes with whole-hearted tributes to the Master and Wardens of the Company for their liberality in bearing the " whole sole expense and charges " of the " Solemnity both by water and land " ; and to his collaborator, Gerard Christmas, for his admirable mounting of the shows.

So satisfied were the Haberdashers that when in the next year another of their members, Nicholas Raynton, was chosen as Lord Mayor, they again called upon Heywood for a pageant, which he provided in *Londini Artium & Scientiarum Scaturigo : or London's Fountain of Arts and Sciences*, of which the only copy is in the Huntington library, in California. So also is the only copy of his 1633 pageant, *Londini Emporia, or London's Mercatura*, commissioned by the Clothworkers in honour

*Shoals.   †Exclamation of astonishment.

of the mayoralty of one of their Company, Ralph Freeman.

Heywood did not furnish the pageant in 1634 for in that year he had the even more responsible and complimentary task of providing at the Queen's invitation, the masque, *Love's Mistress*, to celebrate the King's birthday on 19th November. There was a preliminary performance before the royal pair by the Queen's Company at the Phoenix theatre, and a third repetition soon afterwards. Inigo Jones provided the scenic effects, and unlike in most masques the performers were professionals, not amateurs. Its main theme is an original treatment of the story of Cupid and Psyche, with other mythological episodes interwoven.

Of his 1635 Pageant, *Londini Sinus Salutis, or London's Harbour of Health and Happiness* a unique copy is in Sion College Library. It was selected by the Clothworkers' Company as £10 cheaper than a competing offer, and was presented on 29th October in honour of the mayoralty of one of their Company, Christopher Clethrowe. It is cast throughout in classical mould, introducing Juno who brings the gift of power, Pallas of wisdom, and Venus of love. They are followed by Mars who sings the praises of Iron and Steel.

> Without these metals, Nature could produce
> Nothing that is conduceful to man's use.
> The Plough, without the Coulter and the Share
> Could make no furrows . . .
> The Gardener's art would cease to be a trade,
> If take from him the Mattock and the Spade.
> In dens and caves we should be forc'd to dwell,
> Were there no Axes made that timber fell !
> Nor on the seas could we have ships to sail
> Without the Saw, the Hammer and the Nail.

Mars then promises his protection to the Lord Mayor
who is finally conducted to the harbour of health and
happiness, " adorned with eight several persons, representing such virtues as are necessary to be embraced
by all such magistrates ! "

The series of Heywood's Pageants was concluded in
1637 by *Londini Speculum : or London's Mirror*, again
financed by the Haberdashers' Company in honour of
the election of one of their members, Richard Fenn, as
Lord Mayor. St. Catherine, the patron saint of the
Company, appears for the first time in a show on the
water, drawn in a sea-chariot by two sea-horses, and
tells how Jove has been so struck by admiration of this
" Royal ark," that he has sent Mercury with a message
of commendation. The first show on land is presented
by the philosopher, Pythagoras, who, in relation to the
four Kingdoms, England, Scotland, France and Ireland
over which "his sacred Majesty beareth title," expounds
the varied significance of the " quaternion" to man.

He acts his whole life on this earthy stage,
In childhood, youth, manhood, decrepit age,
The very day that doth afford him light
Is morning, the meridian, evening, night.
Four seasons still successively appear,
Which put together make a complete year,
The earth, with all the Kingdoms therein guided,
Is into four distinguish'd parts divided.
The four winds from the world's four quarters blow,
Eurus, Favonius, Auster, Aquilo.
All moral virtues we in four include
As prudence, justice, temperance, fortitude,
Court, city, camp and country, the four C's,
Which represent to us the four degrees
Requir'd in every fair and flourishing land ;
Subtract but one, a Kingdom cannot stand.

In a further show the City of London is represented by an imperial fort from which Bellona, Goddess of War, addresses the Lord Mayor, himself of military rank.

> You have been in this City ('tis known well)
> A soldier, captain and a colonel,
> And now in times fair progress, to crown all,
> Of this metropolis chief general.
> You of this emblem, which this day we bring,
> To represent the Chamber of the King,
> Are the prime governor : a royal fort.

The final show, from which the pageant took its title, was decorated with glasses of all sorts, " the persons upon or about it are beautiful children, every one of them expressing their natures and conditions in the impresaes of their shields." Opsis or Sight points the moral to other great cities.

> For London's self, if they shall first begin
> To examine her without, and then within,
> What architecture, palaces, what bowers,
> What citadels, what turrets, and what towers !
>
> *   *   *   *   *
>
> Then her cathedrals, temples now repairing,
> An act of true devotion, no man sparing
> His helping hand ; and many, 'tis well known,
> To further God's house have forgot their own.
> Unto her outward shape I do not prize her,
> But let them come within to anatomize her.
> Her *Praetor*, scarlet Senate, Liveries,
> The ordering of her brave Societies.
> Divine Astraea here in equal scale
> Doth balance Justice, Truth needs not look pale.

Among Heywood's gifts was not that of prophecy or he would not have saluted as " the Chamber of the King " his capital city which in a few years was to be the centre of hostility to him. But in this series of pageants he found an appropriate vent for the display of his civic patriotism, his versatile ingenuity and his encyclopaedic lore.

During the years in which Heywood was furnishing his mayoral pageants he was also producing, alone or in collaboration, some new plays or publishing others written at earlier dates. Their plots are generally more fantastic and less healthy in tone than those in Heywood's previously issued plays, and with one exception, on account of its historical associations, they may be briefly noticed here.*

The Royal King and the Loyal Subject, acted by the Queen's Company, was not printed till 1637 but the epilogue speaks of it as an old play. In it a jealous King humiliates, with wellnigh tragic consequences, a loyal Marshal who has saved his life in battle. In *A Challenge for Beauty*, acted by the King's Company, and printed in 1636, it is a jealous queen of Portugal who ill treats a noble courtier till she finally submits to his love for an Englishwoman, whose beauty rivals her own. In *A Maidenhead Well Lost*, acted by the Queen's Company, and printed in 1634, Lauretta takes the place of the unchaste Julia on the night of her marriage to the Prince of Florence, and wins his hand.

Fortune by Sea and Land, not published till 1655, bears the names of Heywood and William Rowley. It combines a domestic drama exemplifying "fortune by

---

*I have given a fuller account of them in my *Introduction to Stuart Drama* (Oxford Univ. Press, 1946).

land " with the " fortune by sea " of the pirates, Clinton and Purser. Dr. Clark has shown that scenes in the pirate plot are verbally parallel with passages in a pamphlet, *A True Relation of the Lives and Deaths of the two most famous English Pirates, Purser and Clinton,* which on internal evidence can be assigned to Heywood.

Another type of " fortune by sea " is the main plot of *Dick of Devonshire,* printed in 1883 by A. H. Bullen, from the same British Museum MS. volume that contains *The Captives.* It dramatises the exploits of Richard Pike of Tavistock after the expedition of 1625 to Cadiz, and Bullen's tentative ascription of it to Heywood has found general acceptance. More speculative is the claim made by Dr. Clark for Heywood's hand in *A Yorkshire Tragedy,* played at the Globe and attributed on the title-page of the 1608 and 1619 quartos to Shakespeare, but omitted in both the first and second folios of his plays.

With Shakespeare and Middleton producing Witch plays it was natural that Heywood should exploit on the stage the absorbing interest in witchcraft of which he had given proof in Γνναικεῖον and *The Hierarchy of the Blessed Angels.* In *The Wise Woman of Hogsdon,* printed in 1638 but probably written and acted long before, the figure that gives the play its name is a witch, a beldame and a bawd, who plays on the credulity of her neighbours and pulls the strings throughout till the complications of the plot have a happy ending. In spite of some amusing scenes the play is lacking in characterisation and grip.

Of greater interest, though not to Heywood's credit, is his topical drama, *The Late Lancashire Witches,* acted by the King's Company at the Globe in the summer of 1634 and published in the same year. Heywood must take a larger share than his younger collaborator, Richard Brome, of the disgrace of working up popular feeling against a group of unfortunate women from the Pendle district of Lancashire. Accused by a boy, Edward Robinson, in February 1634, of Satanic practices, seventeen of them were found guilty and imprisoned in Lancaster Castle. The King on 30th June issued a pardon to them ; but meanwhile several had died in prison, and the others, though not executed, remained in confinement. It was after this that the play was performed.

Before the witches appear we hear of some of the results of their black art. They spoil a hunt by making a hare vanish ; they turn topsy-turvy the normal order in a family where the father

> In all obedience kneels unto his son ;
> He with an austere brow commands his father.
> The wife presumes not in the daughter's sight
> Without a prepared curtsey ; the girl, she
> Expects it as a duty, chides her mother,
> Who quakes and trembles at each word she speaks.

At the beginning of Act IV they appear under the names of Meg, Maud and Gilian, though later they are called by the names of three of the accused women. They sing and dance to weird strains. Their chief achievement is to draw into league with them Mistress Generous, wife of a high-minded, hospitable squire like Frankford, and equally devoted to his wife.

> I know her a good woman and well bred,
> Of an unquestion'd carriage, well reputed
> 'Mongst her neighbours, reckoned with the best.

But unknown to him she rides to meet the witches on his grey horse, and when Robin the groom reveals this and Generous forbids him to bridle the horse for her, she turns him into a horse and puts the bridle on him. Further strange transformations at last compel Generous to ask her if she is a witch, and she confesses, " I am."

Gen.　　　With that word I am thunderstruck,
　　　　　And know not what to answer, yet resolve me,
　　　　　Hast thou made any contract with that fiend,
　　　　　The enemy of Mankind ?
Mrs. Gen.　O, I have.
Gen.　　　What and how far ?
Mrs. Gen.　I have promised him my soul.

Yet she believes that by showing repentance both towards Heaven and him she may win pardon. And Heywood's procession of forgiving husbands, Shore, Frankford, and Wincott is joined by Generous.

　　　　　Well I do remember, wife,
　　　　When I first took thee, 'twas for good and bad.
　　　　O change they bad to good, that I may keep thee,
　　　　As when we passed our faiths till Death us severs.
　　*　　　*　　*　　*　　*
　　　　Only this much remember, thou had'st extermin'd
　　　　Thyself out of the blest society
　　　　Of saints and angels, but on thy repentance
　　　　I take thee to my bosom once again.

It is a blow after this that Mrs. Generous again falls from grace, and her husband feels compelled to deliver her to justice. Heywood can allow of repentance and pardon for wives who have been faithless but not ultimately for one who has sold herself to the powers of evil.

The contrast between the close of *The Late Lancashire Witches* and *A Woman Killed with Kindness* may perhaps be seen as symptomatic of a change in Heywood's attitude towards his contemporary world in the last years of his life. In them he seems not to have been chiefly devoted to play-writing or poetic composition. As the tension between the King and Parliament increased he turned more and more to political and religious pamphleteering, with a growing leaning to the more moderate opposition side. But fortunately he did not live to see the outbreak of the Civil War in 1642. The Register of St. James's Church, Clerkenwell, records the burial in the Church on 16th August, 1641, of " Thomas Heywood, Poet."

This single-word epitaph is in striking contrast with Lamb's well-known verdict upon Heywood as " a prose Shakespeare." Lamb's critical judgments are usually so apt that one hesitates to question them. But this implies a more pedestrian quality in Heywood's best work than, in my opinion, it exhibits. Lamb, of course, in making his comparison was thinking only of Heywood as a dramatist. I doubt if he knew of, or had read any part of, *Troia Britannica* or *The Hierarchy of the Blessed Angels*. In them, in their highest flights, Heywood had justly earned the title of poet.

But even if we confine our scrutiny to the plays alone, a plea can be entered against an unqualified acceptance

of Lamb's verdict. There is a true vein of poetry in the
lyrical declamations of the Crusaders before the walls
of Jerusalem ; in Frankford's lament that Time can
never be recalled, and in his inspired forgiveness of his
erring wife ; in the gay vignette of gallants flaunting
it in Plymouth before sailing with Essex to the Azores ;
and in the tender loyalty with which Bess cherishes her
lover's picture. And at times his dialogue glows with a
spiritual warmth rare in the Elizabethan theatre.

It is true that he shows no great depth of characterisation, and that there is no sufficient justification for
the surprising changes of conduct in some of his
dramatis personae. But he is a master throughout of lucid
and easily intelligible speech which, in my opinion,
is one of the greatest assets of a writer for the stage in
the Elizabethan or any other period. Of course, he
wrote far too much—all was fish that came to his net.
When it was said of Shakespeare that he never blotted
a line and Jonson acidly commented, " Would he had
blotted a thousand " ; this would have aptly fitted
Heywood. But just on that account he was perhaps the
most typical of all the Elizabethan writers. It was an
age almost intoxicated by the richness of its acquisitions
and experiences—the rediscovered treasures of antiquity, the newly found lands beyond the oceans, the
achievements in architecture, music and science. God's
plenty, even to superfluity, is the hall-mark of all its
representative figures. But we identify its loftiest spirits,
Marlowe, Shakespeare, Spenser, Chapman, Webster,
Bacon with specialised achievement in some particular
form. It is just because Heywood stands in the next
rank and throughout a long life wrote ceaselessly in
drama, verse and prose, and for gain rather than glory

winged his flight—yet scarcely ever without some touches of the Elizabethan magnetism—that he may claim to hold up, in a different sense from that implied by Hamlet, "to the body of the time his form and pressure."

INDEX